CARING FOR RED

Caring for Red

A Daughter's Memoir

Mindy Fried

Vanderbilt University Press

NASHVILLE

Nashville, Tennessee 37235

First printing 2016

This book is printed on acid-free paper.
Manufactured in the United States of America

Library of Congress Cataloging-in-Publication Data on file
LC control number 2016006368
LC classification number HQ1063.6. F74 2016
Dewey class number 306.874

ISBN 978-0-8265-2115-6 (hardcover)
ISBN 978-0-8265-2116-3 (paperback)
ISBN 978-0-8265-2117-0 (ebook)

To Peter and Sasha, whose love sustains me, and to my sister, Lorrie, who was an amazing partner in caring for our dad. I love you all deeply.

Contents

Illustrations

Acknowledgments

I'm grateful that my father lived as long as he did. We had a complex and rich relationship, and by the time he finally died, I felt able to handle the loss. But handling the loss of a parent is not a solo act. Throughout my year of caring for Red, I felt bathed in the love of my family—including my husband and daughter, my loving sister and wise brother-in-law, and my incredibly generous cousins, with whom I reconnected while we were caring for our dying parents. Thank you to all of these family members who sustained me and gave me perspective on what could have been a dismal time. I also want to thank my father's friends, including those in the theater and the progressive political worlds, folks from SUNY Buffalo State and University at Buffalo, and many more. You guys were my rock every weekend I was in Buffalo. I discovered, through spending time with all of you, what a fantastic universe of friends my father had, and you opened your arms to me, for which I will be ever grateful.

I began writing this memoir as short blog posts in *Mindy's Muses* that helped me let off steam. But after my father died, I had this great idea—I'd just weave them all together and call it a book. Alas, that is not how it worked. When I went back and read the blog posts, I realized that there was so much I hadn't written. Writing this book allowed me to sustain my relationship with my dad—even though he wasn't physically in the room—to work through some of the tough stuff, and to consider what, if anything, I had learned from my caregiving experience that might be helpful to others.

The story initially came out in fragments, as I began to relive the previous year of caregiving. Then it struck me that what linked the stories together was the stability of Harmony Village. My sincere thanks to all the staff—nurses, aides, food workers, recreation workers, and others—who lovingly cared for my father and made his final year as pleasant as possible. Quality Assisted Living is not only for the elders; it is also for their loved ones. Thank you also to all the caregivers we brought in to be with my father, initially by day, but toward the end, by day and night. Knowing they were there made it possible for me to juggle my paid work with caregiving labor, and to feel certain that he was safe.

Thank you to a number of people who read very early versions of the manuscript and gave me excellent feedback. They include Kathleen Betsko, Roz Cramer, Mark Fried, Liz Hay, Dar Hummert-Pickering, Lorrie Rabin, Claire Reinelt, Debra Osnowitz, and Lynda Stephens. Thanks to Michael Ames for sharing his responses to some of the stories, and especially for the interesting notes he wrote to me while he was reviewing the manuscript. I figured that he either liked it or that he was trying to kindly let me down. I'm glad it was the former! This story was so close to me that I couldn't tell if it would resonate with people who didn't know me or my family. I'm grateful to the two incredibly thoughtful outside readers, Meika Loe and Carol Levine, who provided detailed guidance for revisions. And a hearty thanks, also, to Gayle Sulik and Peter Snoad, who reviewed the manuscript in its penultimate draft and provided me with insightful feedback. All of your sharp eyes improved this story, but it's still on me as to whether it resonates with readers. Finally, thank you to Brandeis University graduate student, Rebecca Nuernberger, who did some eleventh-hour research on medication management and costs associated with assisted living.

CARING FOR RED

I

Independent but Vulnerable

CARING FOR A FRAIL ELDER PARENT

Celebrating My Father

My father missed five of his birthday parties, each scheduled on different days of his birthday week, and he had been looking forward to them. The first party was meant to be with a colorful group of friends from his theater world, including actors and writers, some of whom he had mentored over the years. This crowd was always a boisterous group, in a good way, trading stories from whatever latest rehearsal they had just come from and railing against budget cuts in the arts or against some crooked politician.

The second party was to be a private one with a lovely woman about my age who was something of a daughter to him, although he had been known to have crushes on women much younger than him. I think she was one of them. She always brought him tasty sandwiches and salads from nice restaurants, thoughtfully selected, and they would chat about politics and the arts until his eyes glazed over from fatigue and she quietly left.

The third party was to be with the staff and residents of his assisted living facility, and that party was scheduled on his actual birthday. It would consist of my father walking slowly from his small apartment or being wheeled by his caregiver to the main dining hall and eating a big slice of a sugary single-layer cake, surrounded by other residents who would all sing happy birthday. Some of them would know who they were singing for; others would not. He would have liked that party, because he loved cake.

The fourth was to be with a loyal friend, who was also his lawyer. For a couple of years, they had been getting together on Friday nights for dinner. They would have gone to one of two of their favorite restaurants, one Greek, the other Italian, and ordered either souvlaki or shrimp with pasta, depending on the restaurant. The friend's twenty-something son might have joined them, too. He was living at home but was on the cusp of moving out and just seemed to like his dad's company.

The fifth party would have been with his two lovely daughters, that's me and my sister, who took turns visiting him over the last year of his life. This party would have been low-keyed but celebratory, and he probably would have slept through most of it because he didn't have to impress us.

Five birthday parties on his schedule, all typed into an oversized chart I made for him—my own system, which I either faxed to him and the assisted living staff or hand-delivered every other weekend. Too bad he missed them all.

AT 2:45 A.M., THE TIME THAT MY FATHER DIED, I was to lead a training institute for artists and teachers in a few hours. I'm a sociologist, and I fashion a living from a small research consulting business with two anthropologist partners and from various teaching gigs, some of which involve travel. For the past year, I had been trying to keep some semblance of my work life, racing back and forth from Buffalo, New York, where my father lived; to my hometown, Boston, Massachusetts; to wherever I needed to be for work, which had, of late, included North Dakota, Ohio, and Tennessee.

The night before the training session, this particular version of "wherever I needed to be" happened to be Kansas, in February. But it felt like Buffalo, complete with a blinding snowstorm that grounded everyone. I lay in my hotel bed, rehearsing the next day's session, occasionally jotting down notes about my presentation. I felt a little anxious, but my father had always reassured me that anxiety is a useful tool when performing in public. Ever the actor, he would say, "Just use it!" As ready as I was going to be, I eventually faded into sleep, notepad still in hand. When my cell phone rang, I answered tentatively. I knew this couldn't be good.

MY FATHER, MANNY, ALWAYS LOOMED LARGE in my life. He was the kind of guy who casually quoted famous authors like Balzac and Shakespeare in the course of mundane conversations. They were either charming or pretentious or both, but always impressive. A working-class guy, self-schooled until he went to college in his fifties, he always carried a pack of 3x5 cards in his front pocket. They were the precious "computer chips" of his time, giving him a system for organizing his busy life. The top card was the schedule for the day. And each card behind it represented the following days of the week. Quotes and important reminders were at the back of the pack. Everything was scribbled in his illegible writing, which only worsened with age. As his eyesight deteriorated, with age-related macular degeneration ultimately compromising his sight, I often wondered how he could read his own notes.

One of my father's favorite quotes was "Do not go gentle into that good night," by the poet Dylan Thomas. It pretty much defined how my father lived, and how he died. He probably didn't even have that one written on one of his cards.

After receiving that wee-hour morning call telling me that my father had died, I called the airline, trying to get out of Kansas despite the hideous weather. But there was no point in trying, and I finally succumbed to the reality that I was staying put for another day. As long as I was there, I thought, I might as well go ahead with the scheduled training session, which was to be held at a local university.

In a couple of hours, minus any real sleep, I thoughtlessly put on some clothes. I headed into a blinding snowstorm with three of my colleagues to drive slowly and precariously to the daylong workshop venue. Once we settled in the car, I quietly said, "My father died a few hours ago," and then cavalierly reassured them that I was "fine" and could pull off teaching our session. No one questioned me or raised any doubts, probably because they hoped I was right. My father once told me that I was pretty good at bifurcating. Like a lot of words he used, I had to look it up before I knew what he meant—in this case, it meant that I was able to separate parts of my life and carry on despite adversity, a skill he no doubt had modeled for me.

I taught the session on autopilot. By midday, when it came to be the turn of one of my co-trainers to present, I found a bench in the back of the building where I could lay down. Desperately wanting to sleep, I became obsessed with finding a pillow. I rushed in and out of nearby offices and was greeted by blank stares from office workers who had no idea who I was or why I needed this item. I wasn't in the mood to explain. Typical norms people follow and absorb about social protocols were gone for me. What I really wanted was to shout out to these strangers, "MY FATHER JUST DIED!" I realized, even in my altered state, that I would seem like a deranged person, and it wouldn't necessarily get me what I wanted anyway. Who keeps a pillow at work, I later mused. The thought didn't dawn on me at the time. My father had just died.

I lay on the hard bench, fashioning a pillow out of a small shirt that left my neck wanting support. It was the best I could do. I was restless and ungrounded, unable to sleep. I tried to find a sense of connection by listening to my voicemail. The first message was from Colin Dabkowski, a young journalist from the *Buffalo News* who had written many stories over the years about my father's work as an activist, writer, and actor. He wanted me to call him right away because he had a deadline for my father's obituary and was looking for a quote. Although I didn't know whether I could say anything coherent, I felt compelled to return the call.

The next morning, the front headline of the *Buffalo News* announced the death of my father.[1] At the top of the paper was a quote from my big sister in large, bold letters, saying, "He was a man with a PURPOSE." What a great quote, I thought; she really pulled it off, and she must have emphasized the word "purpose" because it was in all caps. The subtitle read, "Manny Fried, a guiding presence to area's actors, writers and social activists, dies at 97." Inside the newspaper, the article read, "Manny Fried, the actor, union organizer and prolific playwright, who stood up to McCarthyism and served as an outspoken champion of the working class, died early Friday morning in [a local] nursing home. He was 97." There. It was official. After an entire year of caring for my father, he died while I was one thousand miles away and couldn't do a damn thing for him.

Even though I had no memory of what I said from that hard wooden bench in Kansas, I did apparently answer Colin Dabkowski's questions about my father.

> Mindy Fried, Manny's other daughter, remembered her father as a man of ironclad will, an attribute he said came from his own parents, who struggled with hardships of their own. "He had incredible integrity, and I learned the value of standing up for what you believe in despite the odds," Mindy Fried said. "I think my father suffered a lot through his life but continued to be a loving and giving person. The older he got, the more generous he became."

One of my father's long-time theater friends, Darlene Hummert-Pickering, was also quoted in the article, saying he was "the patriarch of the Western New York theater world, a man who mentored dozens of playwrights." Others were quoted as well, referring to the many people and communities he touched.

DURING THE FINAL YEAR OF HIS LIFE, and despite the family's initial reticence, my father lived in a high-quality assisted living facility. It was not a perfect institution, but he had a small, cozy private apartment and encountered a bevy of staff on a daily basis, including caring nurses and aides, recreation coordinators and food workers, and receptionists and handymen. During this final year, he fluctuated between fighting for his life and succumbing to utter exhaustion, wishing it was all over.

As an adult child, I was my father's companion in this process. Like many adult children who care for their elderly parents, I had a complexity of emotions about my father. At times I had to suspend feelings of frustration or anger at the narcissistic man who wasn't always a great listener; the man who could be a snobbish intellectual, intolerant of others who didn't think like him; and yet, an imperfect man whom I loved dearly. Throughout his final year, I tried to be my best self as his daughter. I rediscovered the primal feelings of love I felt for my father and was his caregiver by choice, not obligation.

Over the years, I learned that the experience of death accrues with each person we lose, and the experience of grieving for one loss conflates with the grieving for successive losses. The circumstances of loss are also profoundly important.

The death of my cousin several years before my father's was tragic, as he was a young man of fifty-four with two young children and a promising future. My mother's passing at the age of seventy-one more than a decade earlier was also tragic, but in a different way. She had lived an emotionally tortured life, and quickened her demise with alcohol and cigarettes, ultimately dying of several massive strokes. Losing my nearly ninety-eight-year-old father who had lived a full life was different, not easier but different.

I wanted to think I had no unfinished business with my father, having come to terms with him and our relationship through years of therapy and personal reflection. But who knew? The most important thing to me was to be there for him, emotionally and practically, to the extent that I was able.

Like my father, I turned to the pen to make sense of my—and our—circumstances. I began writing a blog called *Mindy's Muses*, where I shared personal experiences, as I tried to recount and reflect upon my life within a broader, more universal perspective. Over the course of that final year, I somehow assumed a "grieve as you go" approach—observing, experiencing, and mourning the gradual loss of my father's personality, psyche, and bodily control. I began to ask myself tough questions.

How can we help our parents get the most out of their lives until the end and ensure that they are treated with dignity and respect by friends, family, and professionals?

How do we handle this rite of passage, this chapter in our lives as adults, as we sort out the multitude of options, or for some, the lack of options, around where our parents will live, how they will get through each day, and how they will die?

How can we juggle their care with our other obligations or, should I even venture to say, desires in caring for our own children, being present and available for our friends, and often last on our list, taking care of ourselves?

And how can we maximize the effectiveness of support—be it from friends, family, or professionals—so that our parents live their final days feeling loved and cared for?

These are some of the questions I explore in this book, a memoir about caring for my father—an actor, writer, and labor organizer—throughout his final year of life. In one sense, this narrative captures a universal journey of exploration because as many "adult children" grow older, we become caregivers for our parents as their capacities diminish and they increasingly require more support and attention. In that sense, this book tells a collective story about the adult caregiving experience. This memoir is also situated in the context of assisted living, a housing residential model that aims—or purports—to provide a homelike environment to elders, an option explored by many adult caregivers seeking quality end-of-life care for their parents.

But this is also my story as the child of a powerful and outspoken man who took risks throughout his life, sometimes putting his family in jeopardy because of his political beliefs and actions.

Caring for Red was not easy to write. I sought to deconstruct the complexity of my relationship with my father and discover things about myself. As I embarked on the final journey of my father's life, I wondered if I could care for this man without resentment or anger; if I would remain strong enough to handle his demise; if I could and would assert my voice as his caregiver; or if I would feel isolated as he faded and, ultimately, died.

Being a Radical Labor Organizer in Buffalo, New York

My father loved to tell the story about his job at DuPont Chemical, working in the vat room. That was the room where the chemicals bubbled in their large receptacles until they were "done." It was a boring job, he told me. All he had to do, whether on the day or the night shift, was read the temperatures on the vats and fool around with a few instruments every so often. Initially, he was overwhelmed by the noxious odor of the chemicals, but eventually he got accustomed to it. Still, his nostrils stung at the end of every shift, and it was miserably hot. High temperatures were controlled for the chemicals, not for the people, so much so that he became very sleepy.

"Sometimes, when no one was around, I would take naps on the side of the vat," he boasted. I imagined him precariously balanced on the narrow lip of a rigid circular cliff, steaming chemicals ready to consume him if he faltered. "Weren't you afraid you might roll over and fall into the vat?" I would ask, wide-eyed. "Never did," he would reply, with a smile.

Working at DuPont opened his eyes to the world of the working class, factory people—mostly men—who worked long hours in difficult working conditions, drank hard at the local tavern, and struggled to support their families. He watched and listened, a hard worker himself who gained their respect, and he learned on-the-ground what it meant to be a worker, a low man on the totem pole. Earlier, when he lived in New York, he had studied Marxism at the Jefferson School, an adult education institute in New York City associated with the Communist Party. This informal education—for a guy who had completed only one year of college—strengthened his class analysis and helped him gain some perspective about the meaning of exploited labor. He chose to become a factory worker, a cog in the wheel of the factory floor, making profits for the company while working for low wages in poor working conditions. How could he organize the workers if he didn't understand their predicament firsthand?

The Jefferson School had its heyday from 1943 through 1956, but was finally forced to close by the Subversive Activities Control Board, a federal government committee established to investigate so-called Communist infiltration of American society. Many years later, when I was in my early thirties, I too joined a Marxist study group, but ours met on Saturday nights in a friend's photography studio. One way to my father's heart was following in his footsteps, and he was very proud of me.

For nearly fifteen years, during the 1940s and 1950s, my father, Manny Fried, was a radical labor organizer and proud of it. After this short stint as a factory worker, he fled his hometown of Buffalo to pursue his passion for acting in New York City. There he joined the storied Group Theatre, where he worked with the likes of Elia Kazan and Harold Klurman, and was called "Red" because of his flaming hair, perhaps also because of his left-leaning politics. As I was growing up, my father spoke to me only fleetingly about his life in the Big Apple, boasting of living in a one-room rental where he survived on a poor man's diet consisting mainly of peanut butter, alluding to a girlfriend called Daisy, who spelled trouble, and the excitement of being part of a vital, experimental theater community. My guess is that his worry about my future precluded much talk about his bohemian lifestyle.

Ultimately, Manny was drawn back to Buffalo because he believed he could make more of a difference organizing workers. I also suspect that living the life of a struggling actor was tough. One of his labor buddies told him they needed him back home, and I'm sure that this must have felt compelling, particularly in light of political developments at the time. When my father was asked to be an organizer for the Electrical Workers Union, it felt like a natural move for him, tapping his anger at power imbalances in the workplace. He was attracted to the struggles his working-class friends encountered in their work lives and in their personal lives. As a working-class Jew, the son of Hungarian immigrants who had battled to survive and thrive in America, he understood well the persistence and discipline and sheer will required to clothe and feed a family on a "blue collar" salary. He had heard stories about the fire at his father's dry goods business in New York City, and he had seen the revival of this business when it was moved to Buffalo. He was ready to apply his analysis of economic inequities, emboldened by his Jewish upbringing that emphasized the importance of performing mitzvahs (doing good for others) based on a moral code of right and wrong.

Labor was bolstered in the 1930s by several key pieces of legislation passed under the Roosevelt Administration, including the National Industrial Recovery Act in 1933, which made collective bargaining legal; and the 1935 National Labor Relations Act, also known as the Wagner Act, which required businesses to bargain in good faith with unions that were supported by the majority of their workers. With this legislation as the backdrop, my father discovered that he was able to parlay his skills as an actor and orator to become one of the most powerful, outspoken union activists in Western New York. Like my sister said (as quoted in our father's obituary), he was indeed a man with a purpose.

According to the Buffalo and Erie County Historical Society, "Fried was an important, even pivotal, figure in the labor history of Western New York." As a feisty union organizer with the ability to articulate complex problems facing the workers, my father led multiple drives to organize large swaths of workers in factories throughout Western New York. When I was a teenager, he regaled me with stories of strikes and walk-outs at major factories, including Westinghouse, Markel Electric, Durez, Remington-Rand, Blaw-Knox, and Blackstone Electric. This was all foreign to me, given our middle-class lifestyle, but I admired his passion and, despite his courage to speak out on behalf of workers, recognized his vulnerability. My father was so good at his job that he attracted the FBI, which assigned a horde of special agents to follow and harass him—and his family—for more than twenty-five years.

House Un-American Activities Committee (HUAC): The First Time

It's 1972, and I am home from college and perusing a drawer in my parents' living room where they store—or rather, seem to toss—old photos. There is nothing organized about this drawer. That is part of the intrigue. Looking for clues about my past, I dig down deeper. And hidden underneath old elementary school portraits and a pile of elegant pictures from my sister's wedding, I discover a beat-up black and white photo of my family. I pull it out and look at it intently. In the photo, we are sitting in the very same living room, but many decades earlier. I recognize my three-year-old self, a little girl with curly hair, the kind they used to call ringlets or Shirley Temple curls, back in the fifties. She is sitting on her father's lap, gathered in his strong arms, which engulf her chubby body. For a fleeting moment, I feel the safety of those arms, which held me throughout my childhood and beyond. She looks like she's squirming to spring away, her body slightly angled; but her father is holding tight. Seated next to her is her teenage sister, sporting thick horn-rimmed glasses, a plaid shirt, and a ponytail. She's looking at me, her baby sister, with a smirk. Her mother, who everyone says is a beauty, sits next to her older sister, but she is not paying attention to the shenanigans. Instead, she looks squarely at the camera, eyes bright, posing like a model with mouth open, like she is saying "I'm fine" but pausing before she pronounces the "n." The photo, circa 1954, is the year my father was subpoenaed to testify before the House Un-American Activities Committee (HUAC) in New York's state capital, Albany. As a union organizer, he worked for the Communist Party-dominated United Electrical, Radio & Machine Workers of America. The photo seems to capture a moment of calm, before my father was the target of government persecution that ruptured my family. I can't help but wonder whether the photo was taken just before he took the train to Albany.

In 1945, Louis Budenz, the former editor of the Communist Party newspaper, the *Daily Worker*, announced in testimony before HUAC that "the Communist Party in the United States is a direct arm of the Soviet Foreign Department" and that every American Communist "is a potential spy against the United States." By the early 1950s, HUAC was on an aggressive search for anyone who appeared to be vaguely affiliated with the Communist Party. Senator Joseph McCarthy became the key figure who frighteningly carried out this agenda, so much so that it came to be known as the McCarthy Era. As part of this so-called witch hunt, anyone suspected of "subversive" activities was called to testify before the committee, not only regarding their own political affiliations and sentiments, but also about those of others with whom they associated. Some of the accused "named names," or as my father would say, "ratted out" their friends to save themselves. Not my father.

Being a "commie" or "red" in 1950s America was like being a terrorist in the contemporary political landscape. It signified that you were part of a systematic effort to overthrow the United States government, even if you were simply agitating for social and economic change through labor organizing, peace work, or the creation of art with a social message. Before the accused parties walked into the courtroom, they were already damned, just for having been subpoenaed. That, in and of itself, was an apparent marker of their guilt.

What was at stake? At worst, being considered a Communist or "Communist sympathizer" could land you in jail. Short of jail time, people who were subpoenaed often lost their marriages and their jobs. They were shunned by friends and family who feared that they might be suspect if they associated with you.

In the 1950s, and again in the 1960s, my father was called before HUAC to answer the now-infamous question, "Are you now or have you ever been a member of the Communist Party of the United States?" He was first subpoenaed to testify about his "subversive" activities in 1954. He was a labor organizer with a union targeted as "Communist-dominated." (Many years later, he wrote about the experience in an autobiography entitled *The Un-American*.) The day went something like this.

My father entered a circus-like courtroom filled with others waiting to testify in front of a somber panel of legislators, and amidst crowds of observers, reporters, and photographers whose flashbulbs lit the room every time someone new got on the stand. He realized this was theater. So he tried to heed the words of an acting instructor he once had who advised him that the actor must portray two selves. "With one self, you portray the character, and with the other self, you constantly check the appearance of the body movements of the actor, his voice, his control of the emotion, his expenditure of energy." So, my father mustered his resolve.

My father was brought to the witness stand by two US Marshals, as flashbulbs exploded from all directions. His family was 250 miles away in Buffalo, New York, trying to carry on, waiting for him to come home. I was three years old, with no capacity to understand what was happening, even though I sensed something was different, wrong.

"Do you solemnly swear that the testimony you are about to give will be the truth, the whole truth, nothing but the truth, so help you, God?"

My father responded, "I do, sir."

He tried to maintain a demeanor that was serious and calm, even allowing a shadow of a confident smile that belied deep insecurities. He was aware that his audience was more than this legislative body; it was the public, his family, his friends, anyone who had the power to open or close doors to him. My father was terrified as he prepared to testify and torn inside about how to maintain his integrity, knowing that this nightmare was creating havoc with his wife, who feared losing her family because of her husband's left-wing political beliefs.

The committee chair opened the first act by asking my father where he was born. He replied politely, "With utmost respect, sir, I would like to know the nature of the inquiry so I may know whether or not this question lies within the purview, or context, of the power of this committee." This infuriated the chair, who bellowed, "The witness will answer the question!"

My father replied, "Sir, I am going to give you the reasons why I am declining to answer this question, and why I am declining to answer any of your questions."

My father's delay only added fuel to the fire. He soon realized that he must maintain the appearance of a sympathetic character in this hostile atmosphere. He must titrate his responses, measuring and adjusting his voice to sustain others' interest in what he had to say. He must slow down the pace. He must attempt to placate the committee, even though his words would infuriate them.

"I have never engaged in any espionage or sabotage or spying activities," he said. This statement only riled them more.

And just as he feared, they were about to cut him off, so he quickly and effectively recounted his position. "The first reason why I refuse to answer your question, sir, is that the resolution under which this committee functions is unconstitutional because it violates the First Amendment to the Constitution under which citizens are guaranteed freedom of speech, freedom of thought, freedom of association." There. He had done it. He had quietly reversed the presumption of guilt and accused the committee of illegality.

The seeds for the virulent anti-Communist trials of the 1950s were planted during the preceding decade. According to social historian Elaine Tyler May, the creation of the atom bomb and the upheaval and aftermath of World War II engendered a crisis that created fear and a desire to seek solace in the nuclear family. Marriage rates and birth rates went up in the 1950s, and divorce rates declined. For Jews, she points out, the desire to repopulate was even more profound, given the drastic loss of lives during the war. As men returned from war and women left their war industry jobs, often eventually to find lower-paying clerical jobs, the message was clear: it was time for American families to nest.

In the face of the Cold War, the Soviet Union was then cast as the enemy, and Communists at home and abroad were the villains. Anything or anyone who appeared to question, even slightly, the political or economic system was labeled subversive, "red," or "pinko commie." Dissension or differences of opinion were seen as dangerous and threatening to national security. This context nurtured an anti-Communist climate.

In 1947, when Truman issued Executive Order 9835, known also as the Loyalty Order, thousands of government workers were required to declare that they had no affiliation with a list of government-defined "subversive" organizations. Carl Bernstein, who first became known for his work cracking open the Watergate case with

Bob Woodward, wrote about his own father's efforts to protect government workers from this government purge. As a negotiator for the United Public Workers Union in Washington, Bernstein's father was able to successfully clear thousands of workers of charges, which would have certainly meant losing their jobs and possibly being blacklisted from reentering the job market.

Describing what it was like at the time, Bernstein said, "An atmosphere of secrecy and fear in the government was one effect of Executive Order 9835, the requirement of orthodoxy another" (Bernstein, p. 205). As a journalist who chronicled the impact of this era, he stated, "In the next two generations, politics was premised on the assumption of danger to our very system from certain people—people like my parents and their friends" (Bernstein, p. 205).

Over the years, I have tried to make sense of an experience that pierced the core of my family, leaving my mother angry and confused and my father depressed, furious, desperate, and driven. I turned to my father's writing, my mother's stories, and my sister's recall to knit the pieces together. My sister, now a psychologist, remembers how hard it was on me, since I was at an age—developmentally—where trauma of this sort takes a different kind of toll. I was too young to understand, but old enough to feel and absorb the danger, injustice, and instability around me.

After the 1954 HUAC hearing, my father was thrown out of the union and blacklisted. This meant he was unemployable, a marked man who apparently posed a threat. No one wanted to be associated with a purported Communist; they feared that the wrath of HUAC could target them, too.

Initially, my father tried to set up his own business selling rings, called the Ring House of Emanuel (his birth name was Emanuel). His politically sympathetic brother, Jerry, who owned a jewelry display factory, tried to help him. But the business didn't take off. After struggling for a year or so, my father became a life insurance salesman for a Canadian firm, the only place, he later told me, that was willing to risk hiring him. He kept this job for nearly twenty years, leaving the house after dinner to drive to various neighborhoods where he would go door to door visiting prospective customers, shining a headlight he had attached to his car that lit up street numbers.

Banned from his former life, and I suppose in an effort to heal from the trauma and aftermath of being publicly humiliated for his political beliefs, my father told and retold stories about his courage to stand up to the House Un-American Activities Committee, framing and reframing the experience to make sense of it and find a way to retain his dignity. Always, in the telling of this story, he was the hero; the painful parts were set aside for the books, stories, and plays he wrote about working-class life and about our family's struggles.

In my father's memoir, *The Un-American*, there is a passage about his family reuniting immediately after he first testified in front of the committee. When I read his words about the chubby, adorable little girl, whom he called Linda, crying uncontrollably, I froze. I didn't recognize this child in distress and was terrified to associate this little girl with the woman I had become. This was his story, his version of what happened, but I knew no other. In the passage, the little girl was waiting in the car with her mother and sister, and she was looking forward to seeing her father, who had been away. She sensed something was wrong, my father wrote. But it was like an impressionistic painting, blurred but real. When he got into the car, they were all together again.

As he recounted the scene, my father remembered the little girl's uncontrollable sobbing, saying, "Her whimpers became louder and louder until they became a wail, until she was crying louder than her [sister]. The sound of children crying became so loud in the closed car, it was almost unbearable." He described himself as:

> Feeling like some eternal father protecting his young against the encircling wild howling wolves who were trying to tear his children from him. (He) squeezed the two girls, all three pressing their faces together. How he hoped that when they grew up and looked back at this, they would say that he was right to stand up for these principles even though it meant such heartache for them when they were too young to understand.

His wife, my mother, barely talked to him, she was so furious. For years, she silently blamed him for wreaking havoc on the family, but she also struggled to rationalize her choice to stay with him, ultimately saying he was good for her. My sister and I were caught in the middle of the maelstrom of our family life. It was quiet on the outside, but simmering on the inside.

I don't recall my three-year-old self. But I do clearly remember crying every day in the first grade. My teacher was kind and compassionate. She took me into the hallway, kneeling down to my level, and asked me face-to-face, "What is wrong, Mindy?" I remember liking her face and the gentle way she talked to me. I wanted to please her and give her an answer, but there was none. "I don't know," I would say, as I continued to sob. And that was the truth. I could sense something was very wrong, but I didn't know what it was.

Although my life has changed dramatically since I was a kid, I still find it excruciating to revisit the experience of this child who was unable to attach words to feelings, caught in the crossfire of her father's choices to take a public stance and her mother's silence and anger about how it was destroying our lives. I feel compassion for this little girl who feels like a stranger but who is sadly familiar to me. How could she possibly understand what was happening around her, *to* her? Of course she cried. There was nothing—there was no one—who could or would console her.

That relief, that deeper understanding, did not come for decades. And later, when I became a mother, I could not imagine a parent taking actions that would bring such heartache to a family.

If ever I question the reality of my story—because sometimes it seems unreal—I only need to turn to my father's FBI files for validation. While my parents were consumed in the drama of their complex lives, even the FBI realized that my sister and I were experiencing the impact of persecution. In one file, an agent reported that

> On February 6, 1956, [blank] advised that [blank] discussed [blank] pending trial at Washington, D.C. During the discussion [blank] mentioned Manny and Rhoda [blank] had learned Rhoda and Manny's children *have been having difficulty with other children who were not allowed to associate with Manny's children because of Manny's activities.* (emphasis added)[2]

Just as my father had hoped his children would ultimately realize that he made the right choice despite the ripple effects on his family, he also hoped that we, like him, would be stalwart in the face of adversity.

But many years later, soon after my mother died, I again cried and cried. Much to my surprise, my father jeered at me to get control of myself. Expressions of emotion were interpreted by him as a weakness, a loss of control. He still hadn't learned that sobbing was my way of dealing with loss. I hissed back at him angrily, declaring the obvious: "I am crying because my mother died." I was furious that I had to instruct him about normal human responses to loss. He became quiet and sullen.

MY MOTHER CAME FROM A WELL-OFF family that owned a restaurant and an apartment complex in Buffalo, New York, named the Park Lane Restaurant and Apartments, which catered to the wealthy elderly and well-heeled politicians. My sister was married in one of the banquet rooms, cavernous and ornate with high ceilings and chandeliers. I attended dozens of bar mitzvahs in the smaller party rooms, where I always won dance or limbo contests. My mother would breezily guide us into the kitchen, where workers, standing by their stations broiling steaks or fashioning beautiful pastries, would greet us with oversized smiles. The management had arrived. But to me, it always felt genuine. As a child, I was given free rein to run up and down the building's winding staircases and through the massive hallways with large mirrors where I would practice dance steps, hoping no one was watching. I was vaguely aware that a constant wave of policemen were welcomed into the kitchen where they were fed otherwise expensive meals in return for fixing tickets and who knows what else.

Unfortunately, after my father first testified before HUAC, my mother's family told her she had to choose between the Park Lane and him. She toyed with moving my sister and me to Florida to live with her sister, but maybe her instinct told her it was a bad idea. In the later recounting of this story, though, my father portrayed her as a loyal wife, choosing to stay by his side. Then he'd add a comment about my aunt's mental health problems—she was agoraphobic, afraid to leave her home—saying, "What kind of a life would that have been anyway?!" My mother, who loved her sister, would agree reluctantly.

In my father's FBI files from 1954, which he obtained through the Freedom of Information Act, he is described as "a good worker, but . . . has Communistic leanings and . . . [is] an agitator among union members." According to the files, "Fried's views are definitely along Communistic lines." Even as late as 1967, more than a decade after the McCarthy hearings, a confidential memo from the FBI indicated that he would remain under investigation.

> Because of his background, he is potentially dangerous; or has been identified as [a] member or participant in [the] communist movement; or has been under active investigation inimical to U.S.[3]

The FBI received its information from paid informants who remained anonymous throughout the more than five hundred pages of documentation, their names and other identifying information "redacted," or blacked out, at times so extensively that the page was literally devoid of information. I found it hard to imagine—as my father's child—that thousands of tax dollars were poured into "protecting" the government and its people from him.

Despite the anti-Communist mood, thousands joined or participated in activities organized by the Communist Party from the 1930s through the 1950s. One activist of this era said, "That was what you did then if you were political."[4] Activists took on issues like immigrant rights, consumer protection, housing, and workers' rights. They were fueled by their experiences of economic and political injustice as workers, as people of color, as Jews. This was the case, particularly during the war when many Jews saw the Communist Party as the only organization taking the lead to fight fascism, inspired by the revolution in the Soviet Union. These activists did not view joining [the Communist] movement as a "subversive act." They thought of their efforts as pro-American—not un-American—and as a means to create a better society. Likewise, my father always taught me that his choice to stand up and speak out against social and economic injustice was simply the right thing to do. There was no discussion of sacrifices.

My Mother and Mary Cassatt

I found a black-and-white picture of my mother and me doing dishes at the kitchen sink (see photo gallery). It's 1954, a few months before my father received his first subpoena to testify before the House Un-American Activities Committee. My mother looks relaxed, holding a dish in her left hand, casually glancing over her shoulder at someone. I guess it's my sister who is attracting her gaze, with my father holding the camera. Or it could be the other way around in this triangular interaction in which only one vector is visible in the picture.

I'm four years old in this scene, kneeling on a high stool in front of the sink next to my mother, my body turned away from her to look toward the photographer. Oblivious to the invisible onlooker, the little girl, me, concentrates entirely on the cup she's drying with her pudgy little hands. If memory serves, I'm worried about dropping it. My mother's open-collar, flannel checkered shirt hangs over her skirt. It looks so dark in this old photograph. My dress, checkered cotton with a high-top collar, mirrors my mother's shirt. I remember it as one of my favorites.

We look peaceful together, my mother passing on the gendered skill of dishwashing and drying to her young girl-child. You'd never know from the expression on her face that she hated being a "homemaker." She looks pretty happy washing dishes and hanging out with me and presumably my sister and father. Kitchens have universally offered solace and connection among women. This photo captures the phenomenon, 1950s style.

In her younger years, prior to marrying my father and birthing two daughters, my mother wrote sultry torch songs and had her own radio show. I've held on to the yellowed sheet music of a number of her songs. Many years ago, I took a stab at singing them with a voice that is anything but sultry. One of them begins, "I said I'd never fall, but now I'm falling after all. . . ." The tune is cacophonous and haunting, capturing a longing seductive passion that ensnares the singer, who intimates a resistance to the object of her desire, my father, to which she has succumbed.

Another song is about her roller coaster relationship with my dad. Its lyrics describe a dissonant relationship, softened by emotion and sexual attraction. It is oddly sung to an upbeat tune, like something from *Singin' in the Rain* or *The Music Man*. "Horace and me," it goes. "When we talk, oh, we don't agree. But when night is long and the breeze is blowing; that is just when we get going. Oh sure, *l'amour*! Horace and me!" Many of my mother's songs describe mournful love and contentious relationships, her creative way of expressing life with my father with all its tensions and contradictions.

My mother also used her musical talents to bring the family together. When I was coming into puberty, she wrote a series of songs about animals. She hired a professional singer and recorded an album in a professional recording studio, and my father was the narrator. I got to sing a sleepy lullaby solo called "My Little Kitty," with loving lyrics about a girl and her cat. Then my best friend, Gail, and I sang the chorus for another sweet tune called "Did you ever get to know a little worm?" My favorite part of the refrain is: "He's got sisters, brothers, cousins, aunts, and uncles by the dozens. Did you ever get to know a little worm?" I loved how our mother pulled my father and me into the creation of this project, enlivening our talents and building a sense of cohesion in an otherwise tense environment, disrupted by committee hearings and FBI stalkers.

Earlier in her life, my mother studied painting. She vacillated over the years between loving the process of creating art and struggling to believe she had any talent. I think she found some solace in her art during the hellish days of HUAC. When I was a teenager in the 1960s, and around the second time my father was subpoenaed, she was a prolific painter who was drawn primarily to watercolor portraits but dabbled occasionally with color and shape in still life. She continued to paint portraits until her final days.

My mother was part of a generation of middle- and upper-middle-class women who had strong aspirations that were largely squashed. They were caught between two women's movements, the suffragettes of the early twentieth century and the second wave of the women's movement of the 1970s, with no organized "sisterhood" of women supporting them to step out of the kitchen.

Once when she was reflecting on her popularity with men, my mother exclaimed, "Min, I'm surprised you haven't had any proposals yet! By the time I was your age, I had at least twenty!" It was a thoughtless remark, at best, but at the same time, she didn't understand the person I had become. Her budding feminist daughter was not a believer in marriage, nor was she ensconced in a culture of traditional gendered relationships that revolved around dating and marriage proposals. In my world during the 1970s, we didn't aggrandize marriage because we had seen so many of our parents' marriages go sour. We were searching for alternatives. Moreover, as long as our gay and lesbian friends couldn't marry, we viewed the institution of marriage as a heterosexual privilege.

Even though my mother's notion of what my life should be was disconnected from my reality, I nonetheless, felt the strength of her criticism. She confessed to me once, "When I was a young woman, I was beautiful, but shallow, and much too dependent on my looks." She lamented her reliance on her looks, but wasn't able to break out of this mindset and felt terrible about herself as she aged.

In my mother's era of young motherhood—the 1940s and 1950s—single middle- and upper-middle-class women who worked for pay were expected to leave their jobs once they were married. Even though she had great talent as an artist, she never considered her art to be a career. It didn't generate much income, even though she taught painting and sold some commissioned portraits. Her identity was equated with her role as wife and mother.

Still, my mother railed against not being taken seriously as a woman and as an artist. The imbalance of her marriage to my father —whose life was large—further ignited her insecurities. My mother's favorite artist, Mary Cassatt, expressed similar discord about women's roles. She is quoted as saying, *"There's only one thing in life for a woman; it's to be a mother. . . . A woman artist must be . . . capable of making primary sacrifices."* For many years, Cassatt painted portraits of mothers and children, but she never married or had children herself. "*I am independent!*" declared Cassatt. "*I can live alone and I love to work!*" I think this artist's indomitable spirit, recognition of women's sacrifice, and adoration of the mother-child relationship resonated with my mother.

There were other parallels in their lives, too. Cassatt began studying painting at the Pennsylvania Academy of the Fine Arts in Philadelphia, where my mother also studied for one year. I never spoke to my mother about why she quit, but Cassatt also left after one year, complaining that "there was no teaching" at the academy. Unlike male students, women couldn't use live models. This is likely just one of the inequities she encountered there. When she left, Cassatt moved to Paris. When my mother left, she moved back to Buffalo.

To be an artist means expressing oneself, putting one's vision into the universe to challenge and inspire or simply to portray beauty. In an era when women's voices were not heard, being a woman artist was revolutionary. My mother's life, like so many women of her generation, was one of sacrifices. Perhaps this was a vestige of the Victorian era when it was considered proper for upper-class girls and women to dabble in the arts, a place for talented and creative women who were denied access to so-called professional careers.

To be considered a serious artist was another matter for women, and a constant struggle for my mother. She intuitively understood there was gender bias, but the proof was invisible, or certainly not discussed. It irked her when the realists or abstract expressionists—always male—won the competitions she entered.

My mother and father met at a theater performance he directed. As the story goes, the actors got off on the wrong foot, my father went on stage to apologize and ask them to start all over again, and my mother found that charming. Many years later, when I asked my father what the attraction was, given that there was such a schism between their two worlds as a married couple, he simply said, "sex." I could understand the idea of sexual attraction. But I believe she was also attracted to his rebellious character, and he to her creative nature. And perhaps the very thing that created tension in their relationship—the suffering they experienced during the McCarthy era—also pulled them together.

As a teenager, I was often frustrated by my mother's lack of confidence in her work. I wanted her to be a strong role model for me, to be a woman who followed her passion and knew she had talent. It was painful to witness her insecurity, as she continually questioned her ability as an artist, which worsened as she got older.

One of my fondest memories of her as an artist was during the Allentown Arts Festival in Buffalo, around the corner from an artist studio she rented. For one weekend, artists of all abilities and approaches lined the streets in the bohemian section of the city displaying their art. I loved sitting by my mother's paintings every year and people-watching. I loved the watercolor portraits my mother displayed. As an adolescent, this was the one and only weekend—every year—that I thought my mother was really cool.

When I was about fourteen years old, my mother included a nude portrait of a young and lithe blond-haired woman in one of her shows. I have no idea who the model was. When one of the passers-by asked if the nude portrait of this woman was me, I was shocked. But after my initial surprise, I laughed and was secretly flattered that I, an awkward teenager with braces and little self-confidence, could be perceived as this artist's model. My mother also got a kick out of it.

I have more compassion for my mother and other women artists of her era now than when I was that stroppy teenage girl. I understand personally and analytically the insidious effects of gender bias on women's confidence. My mother was trying to grow as a painter at a time when society didn't value the work of women artists and, within the microcosm of that society, in a family that expected her to have dinner on the table every night. (No wonder she hated to cook!) The Mexican painter Frida Kahlo once said, "Painting completed my life." I think my mother felt the same way even though she never achieved traditional "success" as a painter. I know that despite self-doubt, her art was her savior.

I know this now. But the teenage daughter wanted her mother to have guts despite a world that didn't value women's art. It takes courage or some ego to think that your paintings will matter. As Georgia O'Keefe said, "*I'll paint it big and they will be surprised into taking the time to look at it. I will make even busy New Yorkers take time to see what I see of flowers.*" Flowers to stop New Yorkers in their tracks! Georgia had guts.

Despite their contentious life together, my father missed my mother when she died at the relatively young age of seventy-one. He lived twenty-two years beyond her and managed to hold in bas-relief the positive things about their relationship. "We had a fine marriage," he would say in a thoughtful manner, reframing decades of struggle between them and ignoring the fact that he had at least one clandestine lover while my mother was alive. Whether it was her company, her loyalty to him, or some reconstituted notion he developed about the meaning of their bond, he loved her deeply to the end of his own life. Or least this is what he believed.

Following My Father's Footsteps

My father was an intellectual who debated with my mother about whether or not he was an intellectual. His interests were narrow but deep. Once my cousin said to me, "All your father talks about is politics or the arts." He loved literature and read classics like Balzac and Henry James, Faulkner, and Mark Twain. He loved theater and quoted passages from Shakespeare or Ibsen or Tennessee Williams easily, with aplomb. He read voraciously, probably more than twenty newspapers and journals per week, and kept on top of international and national politics. He always had an opinion, and usually expressed it with great certitude. He was dismissive of any artistic creation that was superficial and didn't grapple with "real issues of the day." What my father knew about politics and the arts would impress just about anyone, even an intellectual. Yet he claimed in every deliberation on the subject that *he was not an intellectual.* I don't think the label fit his self-image as a labor leader.

When I was younger, I counted on my father to explain any and everything political to me. For example, I asked, "Why did the US get into Vietnam?" He rattled off the entire history of the region. Half the time, I couldn't understand what he was saying. He never dumbed down his answers, not even to children. At a young age, I decided that my father was always right and boldly adopted his positions. Sometimes this got me into trouble.

In high school I was one of two kids who publicly opposed the Vietnam War. As my father had done, I too wanted to take a stance. The problem came when my adolescent friends—who only several years later, in the height of the anti-Vietnam movement, staunchly opposed the war—challenged my opposition and asked me to substantiate my position. Because I didn't understand the complicated analysis my father had ostensibly taught me, all I could say was the part of my father's argument I did comprehend, that the US had no right to be in Vietnam because it was a civil war. But really, if I had been honest, I would have just said, I know I'm right because my father told me so. And I believed that.

In the 1960s, my father took me to rallies and meetings that I found dull and uninspiring. Each person seemed to drone on and on, using language I didn't understand and talking about issues that were far from my experience. Later, in the car ride home, my father would try to explain what they were talking about, but it was still just words, complicated ones that I felt too stupid to understand. I once asked him why everyone had to talk so much in those meetings. He told me it was important for them to express their opinions. Only later did I understand why. In the hundreds of meetings I've led, I always made sure everyone had a voice and had the chance to express it.

Rallies were equally confounding to me when I was young. At one large demonstration we attended when I was thirteen years old, my father suddenly began gesticulating wildly to the man next to us, shouting, "This man is an informant!" It was one thing to be in a meeting where my father was clearly respected and in charge. But to shout in public like a crazy person? As a teenager, I was horrified and embarrassed. I shrank back in embarrassment, wishing I could disappear. But I kept my thoughts to myself, waiting to see what would happen. Later, my father explained to me that the informant was an FBI agent who had been following him for years. He didn't think twice about outing the man in public because, to my father, it was the right thing to do. But nothing happened. No one joined in, nor did anyone question him. On that day, as on many days afterward, I wondered if my father was paranoid or if his assertion was true.

A growing ambivalence toward my father surfaced during my teen years. I was proud of him, but annoyed with his need to be the center of attention. His dogmatic stance on issues cut me out of the conversation, rendering me speechless. I believed that I was not nearly as smart or informed or articulate as my father and that the only way to connect with him was to aspire to be like him, to follow his dreams, his politics, his passions, and to speak his language.

As I tried to be my father's intellectual equal, I also felt his emotional vulnerability. I had seen and felt his suffering. I wanted to protect him. Helping to ease his emotional damage became my challenge and a way to feel close to him, even if I couldn't match his intellect. This was my comfort zone, in our father-daughter dance.

It took many years before I saw my father as a fully complex human being, powerful as well as flawed. Through involvement in the Women's Movement of the 1970s, I began to discover my voice, separate from my desire for his approval. Even though I began learning how to be forceful and hold my ground in the testosterone-filled conversations I encountered every day, I discovered that I wasn't alone in my insecurities. Within the context of a society that silences women and elevates men, I began to see my father's power and authority as oppressive, his inability to hear other people's opinions as shortsighted and trivializing. At the same time, I was torn because we were very close emotionally. Of my two parents, he was actually the more stable one. And despite his flaws, he loved me deeply.

Although I was learning to be more assertive, my father would often cut me off when we were discussing politics, only to further his argument or opinion. If I told him I wasn't finished talking, he would reply in an agitated tone, "I already know what you're going to say." That really pissed me off. I don't like being argumentative. But I felt I had no choice, so I'd yell back at him, "NO, I'M NOT DONE!" He would then listen begrudgingly, waiting impatiently until he could retort. Eventually, I learned to hold my ground, but finding and using my voice was a process that took years.

Around the time I graduated from college, my father decided to go back to college himself. Of the nine children in his family, only two received financial support to get a college degree. He wasn't one of them and so harbored a secret sense of inadequacy. Yet, by the time he decided to pursue his college education, he had gained enough confidence and direction to know he wanted a degree in English and that someday he wanted to teach. Starting with only one year under his belt, he finished his bachelor's degree, getting credit along the way for "life experience." Then he went on to get his PhD. Upon graduation, he was hired to teach composition and creative writing at the local state college, thereby starting a new career when he was in his sixties. I still find inspiration from this story, both because my father was so driven and because age wasn't an impediment to the pursuit of his dreams. These attributes have guided many of my life choices as I've aged.

Caring for Manny: The Chore of Living Independently

After my mother died in 1989, for more than twenty years, my father lived by himself in a small, single-family house in a middle-class neighborhood in Buffalo, New York. My parents moved into that house when I left for college, maintaining a bedroom to which they had hoped I'd someday return. My mother asked me what colors I wanted it painted. "Pink and orange," I said, choosing colors that would bring life and vitality to a household I only knew as depressing, and where I hoped I would never have to return.

Living alone in that house suited my father for a long time. He was near the university where he taught, the theaters where he acted, and the bars and clubs where he met friends. After my mother died, he appeared to carry on as usual. He may have felt less guilt about the on-and-off girlfriend he'd had, presumably unbeknownst to my mother.

Even though he carried on, my father, like many elderly people, was lonely, resistant to change, at ease with the familiar, afraid of alternatives. Over the years when my father's health was still intact, my sister and I would suggest that he live in one of our cities, offering to help him settle into a nearby apartment. Neither of us had easily accessible homes. But the draw of staying in his hometown was too strong. Buffalo was where he was known and respected, where he was a local hero with a theater named after him, and where he had influenced so many people over so many years.

Despite his public persona as a powerful labor leader in labor's heyday and as a successful local playwright, my father was a shy man whose experience of political persecution haunted him the rest of his life. He often felt excluded and shunned. But he liked the house he lived in. It was a known entity with its seventies decor and fifties-style drapes that created a dark, cloistered feeling; perhaps what mattered the most was that he could easily navigate its simple layout. It had a small bedroom with an adjacent bathroom, a kitchen that became "command central" for phone-calling and note-taking, and a dining room table where he did his writing.

My father remained active and worked into his nineties, but he dreaded weekends because he was afraid to be alone and miserable. In preparation for the two-day time vacuum, he'd pull out his tattered directory of friends and go "down the list," as he would say, looking for someone to share lunch or dinner, or perhaps a play.

Every year, a close friend who spent summers in Buffalo arrived like clockwork, which seemed to cheer my father up. Unfortunately, given that she lived out of town, that relationship was "seasonal." During the year, if a friend didn't call back right away, it only reinforced his sense of insignificance. "They have their own lives," he'd say, hiding disappointment and sadness.

However, a number of friends came to his rescue—or his perception of rescue—inviting him to the theater, or picnics, or parties. Even when they all had a good time, my father surmised they were doing him a favor. I remember learning about Piaget's concept of "object constancy" in an introductory college psychology class—that is, the notion that even when people cannot be seen or heard, they continue to exist. Somehow, and I'm not sure why, my father didn't complete this stage of development. When he wasn't in someone else's presence, they seemed to disappear, at least in his own mind.

When our father's health declined, my sister and I began calling him every day to chat. We wanted to fill the gap and let him know he was loved. I always had the feeling I was caring for a wounded soul, his outer persona so out of sync with the person he was on the inside. To me this vulnerability was evident. Maybe others glimpsed it and that was part of his appeal, although they weren't able to articulate it.

My sister and I both lived in other cities, and calling our father daily seemed like the least we could do. We also wanted to monitor his health. We knew that his eyesight was failing and that he'd had a few minor falls. He rarely complained about these problems, but sometimes they involved short hospital visits that he downplayed. He always seemed to bounce back. That was the amazing thing about him.

After my father turned ninety, he began to accrue a number of awards for life-long achievements. One of his favorites was from the Buffalo Chamber of Commerce, an organization that openly disagreed with him during the McCarthy days. He viewed that award as vindication, proof of changing times and his acceptance as a leader in the city. Other awards came for mentoring young playwrights, for being a strong spokesperson for peace and civil rights, and for his contribution to the arts. You name it. He both loved and felt embarrassed about getting so many awards. "That's what you get when you live as long as I do!" he would say, to diffuse his discomfort.

My father's gratification in receiving these awards was tempered by the real humility of a working-class guy who could not have imagined such success. Although he seemed to enjoy the adulation at each award ceremony, it seemed to fade in his mind within days, as did other successes. He seemed to question incessantly who he was and what he contributed to the universe over his long life.

Staying in Buffalo with his theater and labor friends and community gave my father tangible evidence that he existed. These friends probably added years and greater happiness to his life. When his health began to fail, I learned how deeply they cared about him. Despite his distorted view of his friendships, his friends were consistently there for him, perhaps allowing him to heal just a bit from his life-long suffering.

I became a caregiver from afar. I talked to my father daily, sometimes two to three times a day, consulting with nurses and doctors and managing a cavalcade of dedicated caregivers who did "my" job by proxy. I supervised caregivers, supported them, and problem-solved. They were my eyes and ears, and I was grateful for their insights. I feel lucky to have shared this caregiving job equally with my sister, with whom I could laugh, grumble, and cry when needed.

My sister and I are part of a growing cohort of adult children who care for their parents. Researchers at the US Census Bureau (Ortman, Velkoff, and Hogan 2014) calculate that the elderly population in the US will increase by more than 100 percent between now and 2050, so this phenomenon will only increase as baby boomers age. A geriatrician told my sister and me that our father was lucky to have two girls. Given the gender division of labor in families, about two thirds of caregivers are daughters like us (National Alliance for Caregiving and AARP 2012). On average, caregiving daughters are about fifty years old; the recipients of our care are about seventy-seven. Our father, hoping to take after his parents, was an outlier shooting for one hundred. He came pretty darn close.

Caring for an elderly parent requires a team effort. Of all the adults who do this work, roughly 15 percent do it the way we did, from afar (National Alliance for Caregiving and AARP 2004). The older our father got, the more we hunkered down to the task of trying to keep him healthy and engaged, and of helping him remember who he was and had been in his life. Ultimately, there was a limit to how much power or influence we—his loved ones, friends, and paid caregivers—actually had.

Well over half of adult caregivers are in the paid workforce, and most of us work full time (National Alliance for Caregiving and AARP 2009). It was not uncommon for me to get a call in the middle of my workday either *from* my father or *about* my father. Whatever was generated from the call—a call to his doctor or a friend who would drive him somewhere—simply got woven into the strands of my other responsibilities. I was lucky to have a flexible work situation that allowed me to work odd times and places. Many people do not.

An increasing number of adult caregivers need some flexibility in their paid work schedules to accommodate the responsibilities they have as unpaid caregivers. If my father had been more with it, he might have recognized that he was lucky to have two daughters who could juggle their schedules to make his life hum. And if he, the former labor activist, had remembered that most jobs don't allow this level of flexibility, he would have been infuriated about this inequity!

The "job" of the adult caregiver is a real catch-all. We drive our elderly parents to their appointments, and if we're providing care from a distance, we need to find other people to do the driving. Whether we are near or far, we often make those appointments, monitor medications, buy necessities, and ensure that our loved one's housing is safe, that their meals are nutritious, and that their friends are aware of what's going on. If we have siblings onsite, we must negotiate if and how that care is shared, and sometimes old family dynamics come back to haunt us.

Caregivers often need to fight to make sure that loved ones get quality care. When something falls through the cracks, it can be really dangerous. This is what happened when our father took a serious fall and we discovered that his doctor, whom he trusted absolutely, was unworthy of that trust. According to the National Alliance of Caregiving (2009) more than half of caregivers have advocated for their "care recipient" with providers of services and government agencies. We did our best, but it was not easy. We care for our elders while maintaining full-time jobs and tending to our lives, our own family's needs, and all the other responsibilities we manage on a daily basis.

Tuesdays with Morrie

I was eight years old when I first saw my father on stage as Brutus in *Julius Caesar*. I was excited, but I had no idea what to expect. No one had prepared me by explaining the plot or warning me about the poetic but challenging Early Modern English. When the play began, I was intrigued but confused and remained so throughout. The actors were larger than life. They spoke in loud, sonorous voices. There was physical conflict on stage, and it was disturbing. The words the actors uttered sounded kind of like English but not really, and their meaning eluded me. While I was proud of my father because he was an "actor," I didn't understand what he was saying. I even wondered how much he understood it! But when the audience cheered at the end of the performance, I was drawn into their exhilaration.

It took another half-decade, when I was in high school and we read and dissected Shakespeare, before I began to understand the complicated language and plot development of *Julius Caesar*. This is when I truly appreciated my father's accomplishment. But I also began to wonder about how he felt about playing Brutus. Was he able to relate to the actions of this character, a man who loved Caesar but chose to kill him for the good of Rome? Did politics trump love for my father as well?

At age eleven, I saw my father play Judge Brack in *Hedda Gabler*, a play that felt too otherly and dark for my prepubescent mind. I was impressed with my father's energy and power on stage but became bored and restless with the play. Instead, I became a student of the audience, watching people's faces and tracking their responses. Eventually, I just looked forward to the end and the thrill of applauding when the curtain came down.

When I was twelve, my father was in a simpler play with few plot twists or turns, one that was totally accessible and fun for a preteen. In this short farce called *Infancy* by Thornton Wilder, two grown-up babies—who are somehow situated in oversized carriages—gossip and chortle about their parents, using shrill baby voices. Contrary to the serious roles I'd seen him play, my father was a baby! Instead of seriousness, he acted playful and silly, something he rarely did in his real life. I thoroughly enjoyed watching my strong-willed, opinionated father become someone he was not. This unleashed self was clearly freeing for him. I wanted more of *that* father.

Over the years, my father acted in so many plays that he lost track of them. First, there were the plays he did when he lived in New York under his stage name Edward Mann, where friends called him "Red," because of his flaming red hair, such as *Having a Wonderful Time*, *Crime and Punishment*, and *They Shall Not Die*. He was most proud of his affiliation with the legendary Group Theatre and one of its leaders, the well-known theater and film director Elia Kazan. Being a part of this theater group, with its progressive and leftist agenda, was a badge of honor.

Years later, he was still bragging about an offer he got to perform in a Broadway show. "The part I was offered was given to Karl Malden, and look where he is now," he boasted, intimating that he too could have been a successful film star. Instead, he said he turned it down to return to labor organizing. And as he often did when telling the narrative of his life, my father framed this choice as noble, unfettered by fears or insecurities.

Of all the plays in which my father performed, I have a few favorites, because of the power of the stories and the tautness of the dialogue. Reginald Rose's *Twelve Angry Men* is a gripping drama about twelve jurors who deliberate on whether or not a defendant is guilty beyond reasonable doubt. My father's character was fierce and passionate. The ensemble was so strong it didn't matter that the entire play took place on a simple stage set meant to represent the jury room. He also played the tormented father in *All My Sons*, written by his all-time favorite playwright, Arthur Miller. This conflicted and tragic character was much like many others to which my father was drawn, undoubtedly because they allowed him to wrestle with his demons.

When my daughter was eleven years old, I took her to see her grandpa play the rabbi in *Fiddler on the Roof*. How ironic that my father the atheist got to play a fiercely religious man. His own Orthodox Jewish father, had he been alive, would have been proud. My daughter was thrilled to go backstage to see her "poppy," still in costume, and to meet some of the actors. The following Monday when I returned to my job at a work and family research center based in a

Jesuit college, I posted my father's stage photograph, complete with long beard and "Orthodox" hat, on my office wall.

Six years before my father died, he played the character "Morrie" in *Tuesdays with Morrie*, a play adapted from the now well-known book of the same title by Mitch Albom and written in collaboration with Jeffrey Hatcher. As the story goes, Mitch, a Brandeis University graduate, visits his former mentor, sociologist Murray Schwartz, as he is slowly dying of ALS, or Lou Gehrig's disease.

I know this story well. When I was a graduate student in a small sociology department at Brandeis University, I encountered Morrie many times. Although my scholarly interests didn't overlap with his at the time, how could anyone not know the gregarious and engaging Morrie? Although we weren't close, I was also friends with all the people surrounding Morrie as he was dying. I had heard many stories from them about the meaningful conversations they had with Morrie in his final months and days of life.

When my father was offered the role of Morrie, I jumped at the chance to help him prepare. We watched Ted Koppel's series of interviews with Morrie, called *Lessons on Living*. It became my mission to introduce him to some of Morrie's friends and colleagues who stayed in his life until the end. My father dove into his research, interviewing Gordie Fellman, a sociologist who was part of Morrie's inner circle, as well as a few other sociology graduate students who were part of Morrie's support team. In setting up these connections, I discovered that, in addition to *Tuesdays with Morrie*, there were Mondays, Wednesdays, and Thursdays with Morrie, where friends came to visit, meditate, and even sing with him.

My father inhabited the role of Morrie fully, and I was happy to have a vehicle—a shared project—to bring us closer together. After all, I had seen my father die on stage before, in Chekhov's *Seagull*, and it was frightening. Other plays forced him to wrestle with issues of aging, such as Carter Lewis's *Golf with Alan Shepard* and Arthur Miller's, *I Can't Remember Anything*; this title confounded everyone inquiring about the most recent play my father was doing. But seeing him die a slow death in *Tuesdays with Morrie* was a different kind of torture because it was a slow death. Perhaps dying on stage is a rehearsal for the real thing, but then when the real thing crept up on my father, he seemed resistant and terrified, unlike Morrie whose trademark was an apparent acceptance of the inevitable.

I, too, was touched with the theater bug. When I was a senior in high school, I got the lead role in the school play, *Cabaret.* It was a concoction of other musicals that our drama teacher, Myrna Goldberg, welded together. My role was as a professor who was researching the cabaret scene. I wonder now if Myrna Goldberg had an instinct about the fitting nature of this role for me, and that someday I would be a sociologist with a major interest in the arts? My character, the professor, began as a stuffy intellectual. But, by the final scene, she had transformed and was doing a full-throttle, solo performance of "If They Could See Me Now," from the Broadway musical *Sweet Charity.*

I'll never forget being coached on how to improve my ability to project my voice into the far reaches of the theater. Myrna Goldberg had me say the line, "The British are coming," while standing in the distant corner of the classroom, starting out with a tiny voice and gradually building it to a crescendo. Maybe Myrna also knew that I would someday marry a Brit!

By the time I got to do my solo, I was a master of voice modulation. I stood on a small, raised stand in the back of the stage at Riverside High School, wearing nerdy glasses and a suit, and began singing a breathy first verse. Then with dramatic flair, I stepped down, threw off my glasses, released my Velcro suit to reveal a satiny purple dress, kicked my legs high to show off my dancing chops, and belted out the rest . . . "*All I can say is 'Wow-ee!'* . . ." I'd like to think that it was a breathtaking performance!

Being in that play was the pinnacle of my high school career. I felt part of a community of actors, singers, and dancers. It didn't hurt that I was center stage and got lots of positive attention, including from my then-boyfriend who was in the chorus. Most importantly, I discovered the beauty of theater for creating community. It is a world more tolerant of difference and even quirkiness, where drama is part of every production, both in the stories being told and the shenanigans among the players. Creativity and risk-taking are welcome.

Maybe theater is in the blood. My father was drawn to it as a young man and maintained his commitment throughout his life. In addition to stage plays, he joined his friend and fellow actor Darlene Pickering-Hummert in a traveling troupe of professional actors she had formed, called Theater for Change. The idea was that theater is used as an interactive tool to address social issues like domestic violence, workplace issues, or aging. A labor-management collaboration between the United Auto Workers (UAW) and Ford Motor Company flew the troupe to cities around the country to join day-long training sessions. They created and performed small sketches that reflected the challenging labor-management issues the union and managers were facing. My father saw the theater as a means to provoke and incite, but the camaraderie built among the actors was so strong that it was the community of the theater that sustained him throughout his life, until his death.

Among theories of aging, one called *activity theory*, developed in 1961 by Robert Havighurst, seems pretty obvious. As this theory goes, it's important for older people to stay engaged when they leave a job or lose a spouse, because they potentially face role loss. More recent research (Kaufman 2000; Rowe and Kahn 1997) shows that, for an older person, being engaged in just any kind of activity isn't nearly as powerful as being engaged in one that the person is passionate about. This was true for my father. He realized that to remain vital, he needed to stay intellectually engaged.

Yet my father's passion for theater made him an integral part of an intergenerational community, which was equally important. As he aged and lost many of his peers, his younger acting buddies became his contemporaries. Because he had lived a long and inspiring life, they also admired him, so he enjoyed the adulation of this creative and loving community, and he acted well into his mid-nineties and went to the theater regularly with these ready-made friends.

One scene in *Tuesdays with Morrie* required my father to dance. His character was in a wheelchair for most of the play, but for this one scene, my father had to get up and perform a grapevine dance, which required stepping sideways, crossing one leg over the other across the dance floor. While he was preparing for the play, he came to Boston to visit me and my family. He wanted to show us his dance moves.

At the time, he was a bit shaky on his feet, so performing these movements seemed precarious at best. He chose to practice in a long, narrow hallway in our house. I was relieved that at least in the confines of that hallway, he could grab the sides of the wall if he lost his balance. But seeing him do the dance on stage, without walls, was nearly intolerable. I held my breath and hoped he would stay vertical, knowing that he would have to do it night after night for the three-week run, even when I wasn't there to will him upright. He had a mountain of friends and admirers there with him, so many of us were holding our breath when he performed that scene. He would live for six more years after he performed in this play.

Over the years, I called him every night to connect and tell him I loved him. But in the year before he died, conversation got harder as his body and mind faded. One night I asked, "Of all the plays you acted in, Dad, which play did you enjoy the most?" He paused struggling to remember their names, and I realized he needed some help.

"Remember when you acted in *Tuesdays with Morrie*?"

"Ah yes," he replied, and I could feel him smiling.

"You were great in that play, Dad. I was so worried that you would lose your balance when you did the grapevine dance, but you pulled it off." He laughed softly. "And remember when you were a baby in Thornton Wilder's *Infancy*? You were hysterical!"

He laughed again in recognition. "That was a good one," he agreed. I could feel him smiling.

"And remember how you were a rabbi in *Fiddler*? Your father would have loved that one." He chuckled, knowing that his Orthodox father never approved of his atheism.

"And what about that musical?" I asked.

"Oh yeah, that was fun," he said.

"I couldn't make it to that one, Dad, but I heard you really sang your heart out."

One by one, I listed all the plays I could remember, and with the name of each play, he quietly said "oh yes" or "ah," as he recalled the many plays that filled his life with a sense of love and pride.

I scoured my mind for every play he had been in because I didn't want that rich phone conversation to end. It was filled with the people and the plays that inhabited his life, contributing to his sense of accomplishment and sense of belonging in a world of creativity and support. I knew I was giving him a gift with that conversation, a reminder that despite his hardships and insecurities, he had felt loved and nurtured in his theater community. I wish I could replay that conversation again and again.

Exploring Housing Options

One summer, when my father was co-teaching a week-long theater retreat for an elder hostel, he met two couples who lived in an interesting housing complex for the elderly. Located outside Boston, Lasell Village is adjacent to the private university Lasell College, and all residents who live there are required to take part in a certain number of educational experiences each year. His new friends talked about the classes they took or even taught, and they raved about the fabulous local theater and musical performances they attended. They wanted him to visit and made a convincing case. So he said, "What the hell." Following the week-long retreat, I picked him up at the bus station, and we drove directly to Lasell Village to check it out.

My sister and I were not foolish. We could see that our father was still able to live independently. He was still teaching playwriting and English composition classes well into his nineties. And he could still sustain a high level of energy in this theater retreat, where he lectured about his experiences on stage and the importance, as a playwright, of bringing the real lives of working people to the stage.

But we were beginning to imagine a time when he could no longer fully care for himself, and by the end of that week, he was totally knocked out. Despite the fact that my father was willing to visit his new friends at their home in Lasell Village, I knew his motivation to continue engaging with them once he left the retreat was minimal. He had used up his energy there, so I wasn't surprised that the moment we stepped onto the campus, he was ready to leave. But their admiration was alluring, and he didn't want to insult these two couples who, like most people who met my father in his later years, were blown away by his intelligence, lucidity, and charm.

So we soldiered on, sharing a meal with both couples in the lovely dining area, listening to them exalt about the food and their fascinating friends, and the active community of engaged residents who attended classes or went to the opera or the theater.

When we went back to one of our host's well-coifed apartments, my father seated himself comfortably on a crisp white couch and quietly slipped into a deep slumber that lasted until we got up to leave an hour later. Meanwhile, it was left to me to chit-chat with these newfound friends, all the while wondering how long his nap would last, and speculating what our hosts thought about the snoring guy on the couch who had been their esteemed mentor and teacher.

Once we were back in the car, I asked my father what he thought about the place. "It would be like dropping me off a cliff," he grunted. As it turned out, Lasell Village had little appeal to him, even with a university of young people next door. With that, I decided to focus my efforts more locally.

When my sister and I first embarked on researching housing alternatives, we had no idea what, if anything, would appeal to an active elder like our father. We knew we had to explore the options, but it seemed so overwhelming. We targeted urban and suburban assisted living facilities, knowing that the idea of an age-segregated facility had always been anathema to our father. He never joined an organization in which membership was proscribed by age, so why would he be open to it now? While he felt fine teaching in an elder hostel program, he would never choose to be a participant. A move to any facility would be a hard sell.

We also knew that staying in Buffalo was a wise move. Our dad was rooted in the city, where he was known and admired for his plays, his acting, and his political work. During my next visit to Buffalo, I visited Harmony Village, the local assisted living facility where my aunt had lived before moving to a nursing home.[5]

Welcome to Harmony Village

Harmony Village is located on Main Street in a cozy suburban neighborhood of Buffalo, New York. The town is sprinkled with fading storefronts, mediocre Italian and Greek restaurants, a smattering of churches, and my favorite chocolate shop, which sells sponge candy, a peculiarly Buffalo invention to which I am addicted. Conveniently for me, the candy store is located just across the street from the residence!

When I first saw it, Harmony Village looked like a faux castle, an ominous red-brick structure that extended one full block in each direction, with four floors and tall round turrets on each corner. I imagined that this fortlike building, which housed about two hundred residents in apartments, was meant to evoke a sense of safety from outside forces—as if any place could guard old people against the inevitable: death.

At the front desk sat either John or Myra. If it was John, you knew you would get a straight answer. A former military guy in his twenties, he was reliable, kind, and looked you in the eye when he talked to you. John was super-with-it. If you got Myra, you were better off taking care of things yourself. She mixed up names and numbers. And she looked at you as though she had no idea who you were, even if you had talked to her on a daily basis for the past six months. I always wondered how she kept that job—perhaps thanks to the kindness of some administrator.

The first time I visited Harmony Village, I couldn't imagine my father living there. I barely tolerated the tour myself. The hard sell of the too-chipper marketing person, who painstakingly tried to convince me that "your father would be very happy here" made me want to puke. I tried hard to persevere. The over-zealous guide led me through the dining hall, populated with a small group of women who were sitting together at a circular table, negotiating the food on their plates but barely communicating. She boasted about the amazing chef and how much the residents loved the food. It was over the top.

Harmony Village was far from a four-star hotel, but she would have liked me to believe otherwise. Later I learned that the food was decent. The usual institutional fare was prepared with care and made more palatable by the affable food services director and wait staff. They were kind and loving toward every resident.

Knowing that my father was a professor, the last of his many careers, my guide then took me to the library. She was thrilled to tell me, "There is a professor here that your father would really enjoy," as if being in a similar profession is the tie that binds souls. When these two former teachers did eventually meet a year or so later, they found they had little in common.

The living room and snack area were located on the first floor.

When we arrived, they were both empty. I wondered why. Does anyone else live here other than those few women in the dining hall? I later learned that life within Harmony Village is ordered with a level of regimentation that defines when and where people can be at any time day or night. There are three shifts for mealtime, during which residents mingle in the dining hall or wait in a procession to get into the room. Exercise classes meet twice a day, old movies are shown once a day, and cocktail hour begins promptly at four o'clock. Residents get to drink Manhattans or Mojitos in tiny paper cups, like the ones you get at the dentist's office to rinse out your mouth after getting your teeth worked on.

Unless you're there regularly, it's hard to see the structure of daily life and the nuanced relations—between and among residents, and between staff and residents—that create the culture of life in the village.

Assisted Living: What Services Can Be Expected?

Assisted living facilities are an odd hybrid of care that, at the most basic level, provides housing and, in some cases, involves medication management or other nursing supports. These facilities frame themselves as homelike and welcoming, a veritable antidote to nursing homes, which still suffer from horrific reputations, often well-deserved prior to passage of the Nursing Home Reform Act of 1987. But the amount of care provided in assisted living varies, and this option is not for everyone.

In a number of states, assisted living staff cannot legally administer medication. Luckily, we learned this was not the case at Harmony Village, where an incredibly competent nursing staff visited my father three times a day to put drops into his eyes. This service, free in a nursing home, comes with a price in assisted living.

While the term "assisted living" has become ubiquitous, its meaning is extremely varied. Some assisted living facilities are very small and include only a few beds. The expression "bed and board" is still used in some states to refer to this type of residence. Others are more institutional and house hundreds of residents. Most assisted living facilities have private apartments, often just a room with a private bathroom; but others double up residents in shared bedrooms and shared bathrooms. Assisted living facilities operate outside of federal regulations, but they must be licensed at the state level. That said, what the facilities are licensed to do and provide varies across states.

Forty-one states and the District of Columbia now use the terminology, "assisted living" in their regulations, but the philosophies among facilities vary as well. The National Center for Assisted Living (NCAL), a national policy organization that advocates for assisted living at the state and federal level, has developed a set of guiding principles to describe assisted living and offer ways for these facilities to "develop and improve services."[6] While these principles are not policies, per se, they provide a framework against which facilities can be assessed. For example, according to NCAL, assisted living should provide twenty-four-hour supervision and assistance, as well as activities and health-related services. Harmony Village's programming certainly met these criteria.

As of 2009, there were 36,000 assisted living facilities in the US, according to the Assisted Living Federation of America (ALFA). The type of care one finds in assisted living used to be part of a stratified system of care offered by nursing homes. But as nursing homes began to focus more on providing skilled nursing care, assisted living facilities attracted frail elders who were able to live semi-independently. Some critics feel that nursing homes may be a better bet for elders because they are more equipped to deal with medical emergencies. But there was never any question in our minds that nursing homes were to be avoided, given our resistance—rational or otherwise—to institutionalized care.

Caring for Manny: The Fall

Throughout his life, my father had the ability to doze anytime, day or night. His eyes would get heavy and suddenly he was out, mouth slightly ajar and muscles relaxed, only to emerge five minutes later as if there were no intervening pause. When he entered his nineties, he started to struggle with insomnia. This is fairly common among older people, perhaps as a side effect of medications, lack of exercise, or possibly a change in the architecture of sleep.

I imagine the construct of sleep as a building with stairs that bring the visitor from floor to floor, juxtaposing dream states with deep sleep. The older we get in this building, the more likely we are to land on floor three instead of two, or miss a floor entirely. And when that happens, the mind is less sharp, and the body weakened. I also wonder if deeper factors sabotaged my father's restful nights, such as loneliness and guilt, or fear of death.

Although I spoke with my father nearly every day, I only heard about his sleeping problem in passing. He was not a complainer. He consulted with his physician, Dr. Fine, who prescribed Ambien, a potent sleep drug. Dr. Fine had been my father's doctor for decades, and was someone for whom my father had great respect and loyalty. Dr. Fine was in his early seventies, but people wear their ages differently. With a father who maintained his lucidity well into his nineties, we were not concerned about the chronology. But Dr. Fine seemed disorganized, and his memory appeared to have major holes. He pondered over decisions, often deferring to my sister and me, when we were the ones needing guidance. But mostly, we were furious that he prescribed Ambien for our father.

I had taken Ambien years before when I was recovering from a back injury that made it impossible to sleep, weaving a wicked combination of pain and despair. I lay flat for months, waiting to heal and trying various therapeutic approaches. The pain was only getting worse. I was desperate for anything that promised a good night's sleep. I tried a variety of sleep medications, among them Ambien. When my father began to struggle with insomnia, I understood his desperation. But Dr. Fine never acknowledged that this drug was the beginning of a long slope downward. Our trust in him was broken.

After taking his prescribed dose of Ambien, my father woke up in the middle of the night to urinate, feeling woozy and disoriented. He stumbled toward the bathroom, a familiar route, but something didn't feel right. His head started to swirl. He grabbed for something to steady himself, the wall in the hallway, a door knob, anything. But he didn't have the strength to hold on. Suddenly and unexpectedly, he collapsed to the floor, which he later described as a violent thud.

Over the years, I had seen my father fall many times, even though he exercised daily and had a strong body. But he was impulsive in his movements, and sometimes literally moved too fast for himself. I remember one time when we were on a walk, he fell and got a gash on his hand. He insisted that we continue, reassuring me that he was okay, sprinkling a trail of blood on the tree-filled pathway.

But this time it was different. This was a hard fall, and his body was heavy and drugged. He was scared and knew he needed help immediately. Grabbing for the emergency button that hung around his neck—the button he had resisted getting for a year—he tried to push, but his fingers lacked the strength. Damn that arthritis, he thought. But he persevered. This one felt like life or death, so he kept trying, again and again. Gradually, realizing it was futile, he began to drag his body slowly, painstakingly, inching past the hallway and into the kitchen to the phone. Then the hallucinations began, cloudy visions of indiscernible figures around him, taunting and frightening him. They were telling him something, but he couldn't hear their words. He just knew he was terrified and alone. He reached for the phone, dialed 911, and then collapsed.

The ambulance workers arrived immediately, but it took a while for them to get inside his home. The door was locked and his body was lodged in front of it. Dr. Fine called later that day to tell us our father was admitted into the hospital. I suppose I hoped my father would defy all odds, this strong force of nature who seemed immortal. This was the story of his life, pushing through pain.

In my journal, I wrote the following entry:

> *For the past six months, I have been deeply immersed as caregiver, case manager, daughter extraordinaire to my 96-year-old father. After a terrifying fall in his home where he'd been living alone for many decades, he finally acquiesced to his daughters' persuasive arguments that he should move to an assisted living facility. I realize that long-distance caregiving has become increasingly common, but until you've done it, I could not have imagined how all-encompassing it would be.*

That night, I dreamed that I was carrying a horse, cradling it in my arms, despite its giant girth, gently tucking its back legs into the crook of my elbow. The horse was safe, and for this, I was happy, but it was just a little too heavy, and I was afraid that I would hurt my back if I carried it any longer. I saw someone immediately in front of me and asked her to carry the horse, but then I worried that it was not being cradled well enough, that its legs weren't being cradled in exactly the right way. I couldn't do it physically, but I still bore the psychological burden of carrying this horse.

I woke up feeling the weight of my father's demise, the overwhelming sense of responsibility that I would be carrying him to his final days.

The second time I visited Harmony Village, my father's health had already declined, and I was more open to the possibility of his living there. My sister and I had finally decided to take him in for a visit. He needed to see the place for himself. It didn't go well. Soon after we arrived, our father shut down. He remained quiet as the persistent marketing person did her best to convince him that he would find kindred spirits there. Just as she did with me, she touted "the professor" who lived at the village, cooing that they would make fast friends. My father barely concealed his disgust with her pandering. She thought she recognized his "type" and tested out other strategies to woo him. She even suggested that he could be the village's drama expert, running sessions for the residents on theater and politics. He almost fell for this one. Later he caught himself, saying sharply to me, "I got her number." He scowled, resisting with every bit of his strength the notion that he might live there, and wondering at the same time if this was his fate.

My sister also tried to convince our father that he might make new friends there. When that failed, we tried to sweeten the deal by reminding him that he didn't have to play bingo or watch old movies with these people. He could have friends visit. He could go out with us or friends to restaurants and the theater. Unconvinced, he envisioned imprisonment, while my sister and I were beginning to see salvation. We realized that he could no longer live independently, and Harmony Village seemed to provide quality care. The problem with any institution is that it isn't home. This may seem obvious, but with a facility that tries to pitch itself as home-like, it's almost easy to get distracted from this basic fact.

2

Adjusting to Assisted Living

A FAMILY AFFAIR

Moving into Harmony Village

Ultimately we chose Harmony Village for a number of reasons: quality, access, and relative affordability. In addition to our visits to the village, we learned a lot about the facility from our beloved aunt who spent a year there before she was moved to a "memory unit" of another local institution. She immediately found her "crowd" of women friends and seemed to slide into her new life with none of the apparent resistance my father manifested. Maybe women can do that more easily, since our lives are often deeply interwoven with female friends and relatives. Men traditionally depend on their wives, who become the link to their emotional lives and relationships.

I once visited my aunt in the dining room. She seemed upbeat, proudly introducing me to a lively group of women who looked interested in me and happy to converse. Although my aunt occasionally complained about minor infractions, she felt well cared for by the staff, made new friends, and seemed to be extremely well adjusted. It helped that Harmony Village was around the corner from her daughter and family and down the street from her former house. I felt more confident in the care when her daughter, my cousin, confirmed that she too was satisfied with the institution's quality of care. Our own observations reinforced that impression, as we observed staff speaking to residents respectfully.

Another selling point was the building handyman who moonlighted by working for my father when he was still living independently in his own home. Jim was a pleasant guy who could fix just about anything. He ended up being one of the important threads who normalized living at Harmony Village.

In August, two days after my husband and I dropped our daughter off at a college dorm, I took a plane to Buffalo. My sister and brother-in-law had already shrunk my father's home and his belongings into a small, L-shaped room at Harmony Village, complete with kitchenette and a leprechaun-sized bathroom. It was as simple as that. There was no other option. It wasn't safe for him to live in his home independently.

Throughout late summer and early fall, although my father's belongings were now at Harmony Village, he took residence in and out of the hospital. His heart, his lungs, and his kidneys were all in serious decline. Whenever I reviewed his medical chart, my heart would jump with the realization that his demise was real. He had congestive heart failure, renal disease, and weak lungs. I spent days on end sitting by my father's side at the hospital, making sure he was comfortable and well cared for, reading out loud *Of Spirits and Madness* by Paul Linde, a book I love and one that, surprisingly, he found fascinating despite his short attention span. The book is the story of a Western psychiatrist who is forced to explore non-Western approaches to treating mental illness in Africa. I was just grateful my father could concentrate enough to be entertained during this crisis. When he dozed off, I took the opportunity to consult with specialists and to speak with Dr. Fine, though I increasingly questioned his judgment.

It's important to make friends with the hospital staff, all of them, and to treat them kindly. First of all, they deserve respect, but secondly, they wield a lot of power. The staff really can make mountains move if they so choose. My father still complained miserably about them. When he told me that the night staff was surly and unkind to him, I pleaded with the head nurse the following day. "This is a Catholic hospital," I said, trying to control my anger. "Their behavior isn't Christian." And then, drawing upon my most refined but cheeky Jewish chutzpah to implore them to "do the Christian thing" and address the situation immediately, I added simply, "It is unacceptable."

Although I was frustrated with the inconsistent quality of care at the hospital, it was satisfying that I could successfully push to improve the situation. One time, when I entered my father's hospital room in the morning and he was still sleeping, I quietly rearranged his blanket. With eyes closed and voice quietly appreciative, he said to me, "I can tell you're not the nurse. You're being so gentle."

He wasn't always appreciative. Another time when I was on my way out the door, my sister primed to take over after my week-long visit of caring for him, he barely acknowledged I was leaving. He just yelled demands at my sister, his new caregiver, "Where is my chocolate?" When my sister reminded him I was leaving and asked him to thank me for caring for him so lovingly, he replied grudgingly, "Thank you." And with a slight smirk on his face, he repeated his demand, "Where is my chocolate?" There he was, my father, the more-than-ninety-year-old teenage rebel getting a kick out of being a pain in the ass.

That night, I dreamed that I was climbing down stairs made of thick slabs of stone, all lined up vertically. There was nothing to hold onto. I kept climbing down the dangerous staircase, but I noted to myself that I was making slow progress. This felt like an apt metaphor for the arduous process of caring for my father as I struggled to find something to hold onto in this new terrain of illness and loss. I had no option but to continue, and progress was measured in the quality of care and love I gave him.

Being by "Red's" side day in and out started to take a toll. I have always had *shpilkes* (nervous energy); I'm not one to sit for long periods of time anywhere, much less a hospital. But I learned to adjust. Going against my own grain, I spent hours reading to my father, being patient when he was impatient, and speaking with nurses and doctors to inquire, or prod, or interpret.

One day I helped him move to a new room because the staff suspected he had an infection. I was relieved on one level because his roommate constantly shit in his bed, and I couldn't take the odor. My father, on the other hand, couldn't smell it. That's an advantage of a declining olfactory system. When I whispered that I was going to have him moved because of his flatulent roommate, my father laughed. He got a kick out of his mouthy daughter. It felt momentarily like we were conspiring together. Despite his choice for many years to prioritize his work over his family, in that moment—and in so many other moments—my father and I were peas in a pod, political comrades, compassionate to the core, devoted to each other and to our family. I was immersed in his world with its odd pace and momentum.

I had a dream I was crossing the ramp of a highway with my daughter. It was dark and I hesitated, looking into the thick traffic, afraid of getting run over. My daughter moved quickly across and reached the other side safely. I willed myself to move. But my legs felt weighted, my progress slow. As I was slogging across, I imagined the feeling of being propelled by a strong wind that would blow me quickly to the other side. Would the same strong force help me to care for my dad?

Choosing Assisted Living

For several weeks after his hospital stay, my father rehabilitated in a nursing home. During one of my visits, a nurse commented, "I would never prescribe Ambien to an older person." When I asked why, she said, "A lot of them, they can't handle it." I resented her reference to old people as "them," but I appreciated the insight. There are a slew of medications that are not advisable for older people; Ambien is high on that list. Some of the potential side effects include impaired motor function, dizziness while lying down, difficultly standing or walking the day after taking the drug, heart palpitations, impaired vision, and upper respiratory infections. As I mentioned earlier, it was Ambien that seemed to precipitate my father's downward spiral. I remained furious that Dr. Fine prescribed it for him.

While my father was in the hospital, I moved into his apartment at Harmony Village, never considering an alternative. I spent my days with him at the hospital and my nights as a new, and thankfully temporary, resident of assisted living. I had plenty of time to think.

First, I was well aware that while leaving home and moving into assisted living may have been unavoidable because of the circumstances, it was still heartbreaking and shocking to both me and my father and, for that matter, to any elderly person making such a big move. Leaving the familiarity of one's home and entering a stigmatized institutional setting signifies the final chapter of their lives. My father knew this, too.

Second, as a former labor organizer, my father understood that within an institutional setting, he would encounter a social structure in which staff would be paid to care for him, and that there would inevitably be a hierarchy within that organization in which some staff may be more valued than others. This knowledge was at the core of his work when he organized workers, or negotiated contracts with labor and management, or led protests if agreements were elusive.

Third, my father knew that he would encounter a world of "residents" in assisted living whom he had not chosen as friends or neighbors, but with whom he would spend his daily life. For him, this was a real drag.

But the big question was how does an "adult child" select a nonhome setting—gulp, an institution—for a frail elder parent? My father was no fool about the peril of landing in an institutional setting. Two of his brothers, two of his sisters, and one of his sisters-in-law died at the local Jewish nursing home. Just the name of that home makes me shudder. Not that we discovered any egregious mishap with any of our family members; it's just that they all seemed to fade with little attention or care. My father loyally visited each of these family members regularly. He observed the care they received, saw the meals they ate, and cringed at their helplessness and the uneven quality of care provided. For my sister and me, nursing homes were synonymous with death. We agreed that our father would never step foot in that place.

Losing Power and Control

Perhaps the toughest part about the final stages of life is relinquishing power and control. Only a few years earlier, I remember telling my dad that he shouldn't be driving anymore. First resistant, he finally acquiesced and compensated by having friends pick him up to go out to the theater and restaurants. Gradually, we hired friends to be his driver to take him to events or shopping or to medical appointments.

Moving out of his home was a final blow, pushing the needle toward the final chapter.

We knew what my father didn't want. He didn't want to live in the suburbs, physically distant from friends, and psychically distant from his inner self. He knew he didn't want to lose his mind, and he knew he had a predisposition to depression. He knew he didn't want to be treated inhumanly, like an "old person," talked down to, or treated roughly, or in an uncaring fashion. And he knew that he didn't want to be associated with old people, because they were going to die, and eventually so was he.

I think about the book *Old, Alone, and Neglected*, which captures the essence of quality institutional care. Author Jeanie Schmit Kayser-Jones (1990) explores the life within a vibrant nursing home situated in a small town in Scotland. The secret, it turns out, is that everyone knows everyone, and this transparency reflects their broader networks of connection outside of the institution. Many of the residents and staff were once neighbors, where they had different—and more equal—status relationships. They saw each other regularly at local shops or at the local church. And some were even blood relatives. Moreover, families of residents regularly stopped by the nursing home to see their elderly parents and friends and to visit with staff. This connectedness provided built-in monitoring to ensure that high-quality care was part of the fabric of the institution.

I left Buffalo, New York, when I was seventeen and vowed to never return. It was the home of sad memories and limited opportunity. I tried coming back when I was twenty-three, but lasted only one month, strangled by my parents' strained relationship and the heavy air that permeated their home, my mother desperate to reconnect and my father quietly gloating that he and I had the closer relationship. I could not have known then that I was feeding into their dysfunction—or maybe just a product of it—but I knew I had to get away. When I think of my high school years, I conjure up positive memories at Riverside High School, which we facetiously called River Roach because it was located on the "other side of the tracks." I was popular then, but didn't know it. Honors classes, drama club, varsity cheerleading. Looking back, it all seems so normal. But at the time, it seemed like a road to nowhere.

When I first returned to the city to care for my father, my stomach was tense and my mood irritable. I experienced dread and felt trapped in a city I had left decades before, for a reason. But then I was happily surprised because I found that I could be useful. I had a purpose. I was there for my father. He needed me, and I needed to be a good daughter, to attend to his needs and to make sure that he lived his final days, months, or who knew, even years, in dignity.

But it wasn't only that. I rediscovered a long-lost cousin and her family who lived close to Harmony Village and offered me a home away from home. In addition to family, my father's friends from the theater, labor, and education worlds took me into their multiple folds, clearly as an expression of their love for him, but also perhaps sensing the weight of my task. Rather than feeling alienated in my hometown, I was welcomed, partly as an extension of their love for my father but also for my grown-up self, no longer the young girl without a voice, but an older woman with an interesting story of her own.

During my initial visits to Buffalo to care for my dad, I stayed in a hotel, not wanting to be a burden to my cousin and her wonderful husband. But they opened their arms and invited me in. For nearly a year, I lived in their home during my weekend visits. This level of support was critical to my happiness and my ability to cope. My cousin's mother—my aunt who had once lived at Harmony Village—was also in decline. My cousin and I supported one another, absorbing the shock of this stage of life with the balance of storytelling, good food, and an occasional movie or dinner out.

HUAC: The Second Time

My life has been framed by my family's experience with the House Un-American Activities Committee (HUAC). It took me years to recognize that as a fact, as I struggled to understand and cope with my sense of isolation, even at times when I was surrounded by people and meaningful work. As I observed my father's response to these jarring life changes, I was struck by the impact HUAC continued to have on him too, even in his old age. And oddly, the experience of caring for him allowed me to see that he was deeply connected to people all around him, and that they were profoundly appreciative for his commitment to working people, through his work in labor, theatre and other realms.

In 1964, the second time my father was subpoenaed to testify, he employed the first amendment, declaring his right to freedom of speech. By this time, he had become a prolific playwright, writing about his experiences within the labor movement in an attempt to give voice to working people. I was thirteen years old, just about the same age my sister had been the first time our dad had been subpoenaed. And like my sister ten years earlier, I experienced friends disappearing, shunning me, the daughter of a Communist. In my journal, I wrote

> *A couple of weeks ago, my father was subpoenaed to come to a hearing under the House Un-American Activities Committee. He figured out a marvelous speech, so as to get it clear to them that they were un-American, yet he did not get himself convicted. He told them in a way that they were intimidated. Thirteen people including himself were subpoenaed. There was some violence. One 15-year-old got locked in a cage for screaming and yelling while her father was on the stand. [My sister and brother-in-law] picketed for the first day the hearings were held, but in the afternoon, they were admitted into the hearing. The second day, the day my father was on the stand; they got in also, because they were family. Also, mother went both days. My father was on the news on TV. He gave an excellent testimonial, and his picture was in the paper with a story of all he said and did. Also the others subpoenaed had pictures and articles in the paper about them. The Committee left in a rush, in order to get away from people who were anti-HUAC. Practically everyone's against them.*
>
> *Tonight a lady called up and said, "Is this the Frieds' residence?" I answered and I said yes. She then said, "I wish you people would go back where you came from." She called up again and I hung up on her. That scared me a little. We also have a tap on our line. I explained to [my best friend] the whole idea about this HUAC and I think I set her thinking straight, but I got shaky and scared. Bye now.*
>
> *P.S. This guy walked up to my father and held out his hand to shake. My father said, "get out of here, you informer." It turns out*

> *this guy told the House Un-American Activities Committee that my father attended one of those communist meetings or something in 1954. Liar. They all lie for the government. We got another call in which there was pure silence. My father hung up on them and we unplugged the phone to get a good night's sleep. But I didn't sleep so well anyways. I'm frightened to find out how my friends will react, and who are my real friends.*

When I reread this journal entry, I saw a young teenager conflicted between supporting her father and feeling rejected by her friends. Could she simultaneously live with both realities? She was aligned with her father and believed in him. And at the same time, she hoped her best friend would understand. Buffering the pain of this conflict was a cadre of people that included her sister and brother-in-law, who were challenging the committee and its tactics. Even though her parents did not allow her to attend the hearing, this child felt the undercurrent of government intrusion on her family's life, through the tapping of their phone and the friends on whom she could not count. There was no escape.

Her emotions were complex and conflated. Anger at an amorphous entity called "the government"; pride in her father's integrity and strength in the face of adversity; adolescent fear of rejection; frustration that she could not act, but was being acted upon. She soon discovered that her friends—that is, all but her best friend—did reject her. But instead of blaming it on government persecution, she internalized the rejection and simply concluded that she was unlikeable. She pandered to those who no longer wanted her around, but they only pushed her away more, and in trying to be liked by those friends who betrayed her, she rejected the one friend who stayed by her side. Two years later, when the two were more mature and able to talk about their feelings, they reconnected, but at the time, she felt deeply alone. I felt deeply alone.

My father, noticing that I was having a "rough time," suggested that I reach out to the working-class kids in our neighborhood. And miraculously, when I did, they openly welcomed me into their folds. Who knows what they knew, or what their parents told them. But soon my social life shifted from bar mitzvahs every weekend with friends who acted cold toward me, to hanging out with my new gang, a group of Polish and Italian kids who roamed the streets in herds, taught me how to smoke cigarettes, swear in Polish and Italian, and flirt unmercifully with boys.

I started to laugh again, and it felt good. A nice Jewish girl, I joined the Catholic Youth Organization, cementing my membership in this crowd. Every Sunday, instead of going to Sunday brunches at my grandparents, I regularly went to a teen dance club where I danced wildly with my new friends. I had a boyfriend named Eddie Baker, whose father was really a baker. And I had a new best friend who lived in a small apartment with her squabbling parents, who later divorced. My friend smoked Larks, drank coffee, and made herself fried bologna sandwiches; and her mother yelled at her in the morning, telling her that she looked like a whore. I was fascinated! This formerly shunned girl was downright popular, and I was having a blast. Who knew this world existed?

In his study of thirty-six ex–Communist Party members in Philadelphia, researcher Paul Lyons (1982) comments,

> Many local Communists recall how neighborhood youths ostracized and baited their children, taunting them about their parents being executed "just like the Rosenbergs" [who were convicted of treason and executed in 1953]. A few parents reflect that at the time they were so busy trying to survive financially and struggling to remain politically effective that they did not realize how much the political repression was affecting their children. Sensitive children, not wanting to add to their parents' burden, often hid the pain and fears and concealed symptoms. [One of the interviewees] notes that one of her daughters only recently told her about the severe stomach cramps she experienced daily throughout her youth. (158)

It was not until I was well into my thirties that my father finally admitted to me that he had been a member of the Communist Party, but said that he didn't tell me before because he had wanted to protect me in case the FBI approached me with that question. That might seem like crazy thinking, but the FBI actually did follow my father—and consequently, our family—for half a decade, employing agents to observe meetings where my father spoke, reviewing documents he wrote, including plays and memoirs, and even observing the fall-out we experienced in our family as a result of his persecution by the government.

When I left for college, my father warned me that I would be approached by an FBI agent who would ask me about his political activities. By then I was tired of his narrative about being so important that the government was constantly following him. The idea of a government agent following me because of my father's politics seemed even more ridiculous, the product of narcissistic, paranoid thinking. So what if I had gone to a few civil rights protests or spoken out against the Vietnam War in high school? I couldn't imagine that this would be perceived as a threat to society! Then, in my junior year of college, a wiry, middle-aged guy named Hal joined the Syracuse University dance club, *my* dance club, where I spent literally every waking moment when I wasn't in classes or studying. Hal had just been hired to run a peace center for the university, and he claimed that he had a brother in a local psychiatric facility. He was an "odd duck," as my mother would have said, an unlikely character to belong to a modern dance club, probably twenty years older than any of its members, and obviously with no previous dance experience. But he immersed himself in dance classes and cozied up to the other dancers. He was out of place, but seemed to be enjoying himself.

And then it happened, almost as my father had predicted. One day, as we were leaving the dance studio, out of the blue, he began asking me questions about my father. I had nothing to hide, but still felt violated. I wondered why it mattered, my father's political history, and I speculated that he had been waiting for the right moment. Still, I couldn't be sure.

So I did some research and discovered that prior to coming to New York State, Hal had worked in California, hired by the FBI to sabotage the Cesar Chavez grape boycott. I was warned not to trust him, with one contact telling me, "He is bad news." And that's when I realized that maybe my father's paranoia wasn't so crazy after all.

Using the Freedom of Information Act, my father ultimately received roughly five thousand pages of FBI notes, with many of the words redacted (crossed out), supposedly to "protect" the identity of the agent who was following him. Some years later, I spent hours poring through those files and was stunned to read not only that the FBI knew that my sister and I were being ostracized by our so-called friends, but also that my mother lost many dear friends and family members who feared the consequences of being associated with "a Communist family." My father's FBI files continued up to the early 1970s, a period covering my encounter with Hal. Since I haven't requested my files from the FBI through the Freedom of Information Act, I don't have airtight proof that Hal was indeed an FBI agent, but I know. The ghost of HUAC hovered over my family for decades, like a post-traumatic gnat that ignited paranoia and insecurity at the most unwelcomed times. And it stayed with my father into his final days.

My father was a working-class Jewish man of strong convictions who was loyal to his friends, and he risked a lot to stay true to them. He wasn't trying to overthrow the government, although his goal was to challenge an economic system that, even more so today, creates haves and have-nots. He was a very effective labor organizer who mobilized workers around issues of wages and benefits and fair treatment on the job. In doing this work, he was simply executing his First Amendment rights to speak out about his beliefs. Even though his choices wreaked havoc on our family, I hold on to the belief that the world was a better place because of people like him.

Living at Harmony Village (Not My Father, Me)

When I settled into my father's apartment at Harmony Village during his time in the hospital, I hadn't even considered looking for another living space. I was also drawn to finding out what it was like to live in this place we had chosen for our father. I could never really know what it felt like to be a resident since, unlike my father, I wasn't wrenched from my home. But I still could get a sense of the culture. After all, I thought, "I'm a social scientist." Living there even temporarily seemed like a ripe opportunity for a kind of ethnographic study. Or perhaps this was my own narrative, an attempt at normalizing the situation. If I could tolerate Harmony Village, I rationalized, I would know it wasn't so bad for him.

Living at Harmony Village in my father's apartment was a great deal. The place was compact and comfortable; I could come and go as I pleased; staff and residents were friendly; and it was paid for (by my father). It was sort of like a hotel, but not exactly. My father's apartment was on the fourth floor, opposite the elevator. This would be convenient for him, but after a couple of trips up and down the elevator, I thought I would go crazy with nervous energy, the elevator opening and closing so slowly that the most impaired person had time to whistle a Bach sonata before risking getting slammed by the door. Whenever possible, I used the stairs. Occasionally Thomas, a spry resident who kept fit by walking up and down these stairs, joined me. He seemed as harried as I felt.

The second night I stayed in my father's apartment, after a long day at the hospital, I fell quickly into a deep sleep. Sleeping in his bed was oddly reassuring. I tried to imagine myself in his life, living in an institution, albeit one that is "home-like." That night, as I was drifting off, I was suddenly awakened by a bright light shining directly in my face and the shrieks of a startled woman who cried out, "Oh, you're the daughter!" I sat upright and shouted instinctively, "Who the f**k are you?"

Any semblance of "home" was shattered as I realized that the locked doors at Harmony Village are not really locked and personal space is really public space. When I regained my senses, I wanted to know who the intruder was and why she was in my father's apartment. With some embarrassment she mumbled, "I'm doing a security check." I didn't know whether to feel protected or violated. Half awake and in a daze, I ran down the four flights of stairs to the main floor to find someone to speak with.

Harmony Village was eerily abandoned at night. The front desk was empty. No one was in any of the activity rooms or in the cozy living room with the faux fireplace. I darted from room to room looking for human life. Finally, I found a lone employee sitting in the snack room off to the side, reading a book. Shattering her solitude, as if I were reporting a burglary, I shouted accusatorily, "Someone busted into my room and shined her flashlight at me." Without fanfare and clearly unfazed, she lazily picked up her walky-talky to find the aide who entered my father's room, telling her that I was the daughter of a resident, a temporary guest.

I later learned that my father was on "bed watch," a security measure in case he fell out of his bed. Presumably, no one told the aide that he was in the hospital and not in his room. This was likely a legitimate mistake, but I was still upset with the invasion of privacy and refused to be the victim of any more potential errors.

Every night before bed, I circled around my father's room, consumed with a new and slightly manic ritual of stacking chairs in front of the door with its meaningless lock. Then I wound my father's "Pilates circle"—a rubberized exercise apparatus—around the door knob to further "lock" the door so no staff person could enter. After all this effort, I still felt a sense of unease rather than safety. I also felt slightly insane. But I was adamant that I didn't need to be watched. Perhaps then I had an inkling of what it felt like to be a resident at this institution. If I were a frail elder person living at Harmony Village, would I welcome these nightly checks, or would I find this practice abhorrent? If I were actually a resident, rather than a temporary guest, and set up this Rube Goldberg device, would I have been labeled crazy? Probably.

The next morning, I went downstairs to get my father's mail, and all seemed normal. The woman at the front desk greeted me cheerfully, providing me with simple directions. I turned the corner and passed two unadorned rooms, one with simple card tables and chairs scattered around, the other with metal chairs placed around its perimeter. These drab rooms would later come to life when Lorna, the activities director, taught her daily exercise classes or when groups of women played cards or bingo or "dice." But now all was quiet.

My father's small mailbox was barely visible within the grand sweep of tiny metal receptacles, all lined up in post office fashion. Unlike the others, his was graced with a yellow dot that made it stand out, perhaps to accommodate his poor eyesight. However, I couldn't fathom that my father was the only resident in this assisted living facility who was visually impaired.

I stood in front of his mailbox, fumbling with the key, as I would continue to do throughout that year, and finally got it open. I wondered how residents could open their mailboxes if theirs were as jammed as my father's, which in his case, was mostly filled with bills and solicitations for donations.

On my way back from retrieving the mail, a kind but vulnerable-looking man who appeared to be in his eighties shuffled up to me and asked, "Am I going to dinner or lunch?" "Lunch," I replied, feeling a rush of sadness and recognition. Just a few months before, my father had told me, "If I ever lose my marbles, pull the plug." So far, he was well oriented and would sneer at residents who were as spaced out as this gentleman.

When my father returned from his hospital stay, sifting through mail was one of the highlights of his day. This ritual connected him to the outside world, reminding him of the important ways he was engaged as a professional and an artist. He even savored his annoyance at the junk mail, and beamed whenever I read him a letter of thanks from a friend or colleague or a former pupil.

There were residents of Harmony Village who were lucid and sharp. And there were the disoriented elderly whose lives were dislodged, and whose conversations veered down entirely unexpected paths. The disorientation could have resulted from an infarction, a mini-stroke, in which the brain is starved for oxygen and the memory becomes muddy. It's possible that their synapses weren't fully firing. I wondered if I could expect my lucid, brilliant father to start making less sense over time, maybe even soon.

Harry Moody

When my father was in the process of moving into Harmony Village, the chair of the sociology department at my alma mater, Brandeis University, asked me to teach an undergraduate class on aging, one for which I had been an assistant teacher many years earlier. I said yes, partly because I was missing the experience of working with college students, but also because I realized intuitively that it was an opportunity to teach a class that mirrored my life in so many ways. I was more aware of my own aging process than ever before and thought it would be interesting to think about aging in a scholarly way. I also surmised that teaching the class might provide a sort of intellectual cushion against the emotional maelstrom of caregiving for my failing father. Preparing for each week's classes allowed me to explore creative ways of understanding the meaning of engaged aging, ageism, caring for a loved one, and ultimately, loss.

On day one, as students filed into the classroom, I wondered why these young adults chose to study aging and old age. I was an unknown visiting lecturer, so my reputation wasn't the draw. Did they think the class would be easy, based on some ageist notion that studying old people couldn't be hard? Were they just fulfilling a sociology requirement? Why this particular class? It turned out that all the students had experienced a strong relationship with a grandparent or other elder who inspired and nurtured them. Taking this class was one way for them to more deeply connect with these personal narratives. I began to see the class as both a scholarly and a personal journey in which intellectual discourse was the foundation, but also one in which emotions were not parked at the door. This juxtaposition was reflected in my weekly visits to Buffalo on the weekends to care for my father, in contrast with teaching about aging during the week.

I started the class with a reading by Dr. Harry Moody (1987) called "The Meaning of Life and the Meaning of Old Age." I personally found this piece deeply philosophical and engaging. But it had been a few years since I had taught in a university classroom, so I wasn't sure how the students would respond. I knew they were smart, but the article is complicated, and as I laid out Moody's premise, I was pleased to see them come alive.

Moody links the meaning of old age to larger questions about the meaning of life and suggests that old age is the "culmination" of one's life, or a "time to size up the meaning of life." He cites Socrates as saying, "a life unexamined is a life not worth living." I asked students: Do we examine the meaning of life only in old age, or are there questions about life's meaning that we grapple with throughout our lives? On a large piece of mural paper that I placed on the wall, students wrote down the questions they had about life's meaning throughout the different stages of their relatively short lives, from birth to age twenty-one. At the end of this exercise, we had a startling mural that captured their insecurities and worries, framed by age-relevant questions.

From birth to age five, students said the meaning of life was linked to the moment. Their focus was on attachment to family and the relationships they were gradually developing with other adults and children. One student declared, "The world is so big! Who am I in this world?" From age six to eleven, many cited disappointments with friendships and sports and school, where they experienced pressure and judgment. Already, they were conscious of stresses in their lives and had developed a small legion of strategic approaches. From twelve to fifteen, they were beginning to question their belief systems and worried about fitting in, as they wrestled with external expectations.

At seventeen they were consumed with worry about their futures, feeling pressure from the many adult figures around them who directly or indirectly communicated the importance of success—as socially constructed by their class position, gender, and religious backgrounds. They worried about grades and getting into college and even at this early age, finding the right profession.

By eighteen they were settled—or so they thought—for a four-year window at a university that emphasized serious intellectual work combined with the value of doing socially valuable work in the world. They were struggling to align their sense of themselves with those values, searching for their particular gifts and passions to pursue. Many were worried about the economy, trying to figure out how to strategically advantage themselves through internships and part-time jobs. As the end of their university education neared, they asked: Am I happy? How can I be happy? What can I do in my life—through my work and through my relationships—that allows me to feel fulfilled?

My students realized through this exercise that they were at the beginning of a journey. Meaning-making is a life-long endeavor, not only for people in their golden years.

Throughout the semester, students interviewed older people in varied settings, including nursing homes, co-housing, and in an intergenerational dance company. One student interviewed one of her professors and a university janitor she knew through her campus work-study job to compare their life challenges and successes. A very religious Jewish student was deeply moved by the stories of her interviewee, a ninety-year-old nun who devoted her life to Jesus Christ. On the surface, the student and the nun could not have been more different people, but they found commonalities through the interview process. Another student was shocked to find that the frail man she interviewed spent his entire life traveling around the world and had exciting stories to tell.

By studying older people, students were better able to reflect on the stages of life that precede old age, to recognize that life is long and that there are many possibilities. They realized that most people face hurdles and survive them. This is an important message for a young person.

Other students wanted to see older people in action in order to observe their involvement in a meaningful activity. Two students observed rehearsals and meetings of the Prometheus Elder Dance Ensemble comprised of women ages sixty through eighty-six, and they attended the ensemble's final performance, which coincided with the end of the semester. The students were amazed at the flexibility and creativity of these elderly dancers. Several students linked up with a program designed to facilitate meaningful dialogue between high school students and elders. They learned that older people want to talk about their lives—particularly with younger listeners—to reflect on who they are now and who they used to be.

By talking with older people, students were able to see that their lives are part of a larger trajectory. This was especially poignant for them. The next set of challenges—once my students graduated—would be difficult, as they would leave the predictable structure of the university and embark on what felt to them like "the rest of their lives." They faced this stage with trepidation, particularly because of the struggling economy.

The process of life examination is an iterative one in which we revisit our purpose again and again, gathering more information that helps us determine choices throughout our lives. Students discovered throughout the semester that, as people near the end of their lives, they want to know that they have contributed in some meaningful way, that they are leaving something behind.

Harry Moody argues that in Western society, we lack a cultural framework to help people make sense of our lives. He points to Eastern societies in which contemplation is valued as a high form of human existence, in contrast to our so-called modern society that frames inactivity as wasteful. As people age, they are viewed as less valuable, perhaps in part because they have decreased their economic contribution to society. Moody points to Eastern cultures where older people are viewed as wise and honorable, but in our global world, even this may be changing.

Moody claims that all humans seek an immortality of sorts. Some people believe in an immortality that is achieved through contemplation and prayer, which he calls *cosmic transcendence*. (Most of my students wished they believed in this type of immortality, saying "dying would be so much easier if you believed in an afterlife.") Others seek out a more secular type of immortality, achieved through the tangible things we leave behind, like our children or our grandchildren, or the work we performed that results in concrete outcomes that continue to influence others. This might include paintings, charitable work, photographs, books, poetry, or letters that affect people's lives after we are gone.

Reading and discussing Moody's article helped me reflect on my father's secular beliefs and how they influenced his capacity to absorb the inevitability of old age. Claiming he was an atheist, my father was hell-bent on making his mark in the world through secular means. And the way he did this was through his plays, through mentoring young playwrights, and by sharing his passion for social and economic change.

In the course of the semester, I chose to share stories about my father, even introducing him to my students through a taped interview conducted by one of his former university colleagues. Every time I watched the video of this interview, I felt like he was in the room, his resonant actor's voice modulating between quiet and controlled, powerful and passionate. Many years earlier, he loved telling me the story of his father-in-law who, much like him, could mesmerize a crowd by speaking in a whisper. "As he spoke, people would come closer and closer, and he RELISHED the power he had over the crowd just by speaking softly." Even though he and his father-in-law were at odds because of their widely divergent political beliefs, they shared this uncanny skill.

The week my father died, I missed two classes. When I returned to class, I realized I was not alone with my grief because my students had "met" my father through the videotaped interview I shared. My father's death afforded us the opportunity to talk about death and grief in real time, and other students shared stories of their losses. During this conversation, one student quietly sobbed in the back of the room. I discovered that talking about death allowed all of us to breathe with a universal acceptance of death and dying.

3

Settling into Harmony Village

Dining at the Park Lane and at Harmony Village

Until the building tragically burned down forty years ago, the Park Lane Restaurant in Buffalo was located on the gracious "Gates Circle," an expansive rotary with a Parisian fountain in its center. The building had a regal Victorian anterior, complete with oversized Doric columns and a spacious bay window. Behind the restaurant loomed its twenty-story apartment building, which housed an overwhelming preponderance of elderly ladies whose coifed blue hair reeked of another era's symbol of the upper class. One of those ladies was my grandmother, a frail and mousy woman who lived for decades in a lavishly decorated apartment that boasted a gorgeous Steinway baby grand piano in the living room. That piano saved me from stone boredom on our weekly dinner visits with Grandma, and lucky for me, at her death, she bequeathed it to me.

One-half of the Park Lane business was co-owned by my mother and her four troubled siblings; the rest was owned by a wealthy great-uncle I never met. One of my uncles worked in the main office in what seemed like an important job. I will never know what he did. His wife worked in the office, too. She seemed far more focused and confident than he was, but she was never too rushed to help me find a pen and paper to while away my time.

My mother had an artist studio in the Park Lane Apartments, adjacent to the Park Lane Restaurant, both owned by her family. The studio was a small hole in the wall down one of the side hallways, brimming with her painting supplies and works in progress. I can still smell the familiar, acrid odor of her oil paint and envision the globs of paint she mixed on her colorful palette. I knew that room only too well because I was one of her models, until age thirteen when I finally refused to sit one more time. I was not one to stay still for very long.

Half a century later, I am thankful for the five portraits my mother painted of me, including a stylized black-and-white watercolor of my cousin and me playing together when I was three. She somehow managed to get me to sit for two portraits as a teenager. In one I look angelic, in the other bored as hell.

My family ate dinner at the elegant Park Lane Restaurant at least two times per week. In the year before the restaurant was sold, we would sashay into the restaurant's bustling kitchen to pick up uncooked steaks, which my mother prepared back home. As a treat, we'd get fudge sauce to satiate my then and still overactive sweet tooth.

Situated between the apartment house and a large hallway with a spiral staircase that led to banquet rooms, the main restaurant fell short of chic. But it still had an air of money about it, a kind of elegance with its dark ambience and sepiated, mirrored walls, crisp linen cloths atop the round tables, and neatly embroidered chairs. The clientele were the local bourgeoisie—lawyers, doctors, and politicians, sprinkled with the blue-haired ladies from the apartment complex who only had to go downstairs to get a fine meal.

Upon entering the dining room, all were greeted by the effusive Peter Gust Economou, the ever- and over-charming Greek *maître de*, who knew everyone's name, bowed to kiss the hands of women and girls Maurice Chevalier–style, and respectfully shook hands with the men. I found his attention annoying and patronizing, sensing that the extra dose of gush was because I was a member of the owner's family. Of all the workers at the Park Lane, my favorite was José, a Spaniard who always waited on our table. He was kind and warm, down-to-earth and accessible, not obsequious, like Peter Gust. My father thought that José liked us because he knew my father was a "friend to labor," but I think he just liked us, and especially me. My first Spanish language book was a gift from José, a picture book called *See It and Say It in Spanish*, which inspired my later interest in language and travel.

A beautiful portrait of José now sits in the Burchfield Penney Art Center in Buffalo, painted by my mother as part of her series of Park Lane workers (see photo gallery). My father encouraged her to create these paintings because he thought they honored the dignity and worth of working people. Perhaps he envisioned that someday they would be visual documents of another era. José looks distinguished in his gold-buttoned waiter's uniform, staring through those black thick-framed glasses that have been going in and out of fashion over the past four decades. To me, my mother's portrait of José bears witness to a man who made me feel welcome in a world in which I felt ambivalence.

My favorite meal at the Park Lane was lobster "dainties," little lobster tails slathered in butter and placed on a bed of iceberg lettuce. They were delicious, and the work it took to eat them made time pass amidst all that boring grown-up talk. No one paid much attention to me, other than to make sure my manners were proper. I especially liked the parfait for dessert, a delight of rippled ice cream and chocolate sauce presented, not just served, in a tall smooth glass. I also liked the side salad, the potato, the rolls, and the crabmeat ravigote appetizers.

A meal at the Park Lane went on forever and ever. My mother always made me drink milk to wash everything down, as she and my father downed martinis and manhattans. Even though I liked the food, sometimes loved it, I never left a meal without a stomach ache. Over time, I started to associate this feeling of discomfort with the act of eating out at restaurants. I eventually developed a hatred for dining out altogether.

I always experienced an underlying disconnect between my mother's world of the Park Lane and my father's working-class identification and politics. I absorbed his distaste for the highlife represented by the family business. I never spoke about the Park Lane to my friends, except for two people: my best friend who loved me for me and would never judge me, and another girlfriend whose mother annoyingly asked me, "How is the Park Lane?" every time I went to their house. Unsure of how to respond, I uttered a meek, "fine."

When we knew the Park Lane was about to change hands, I brought my best friend to the restaurant every week for that final year. We had a blast. This was the only time I really enjoyed being there without experiencing any conflict, knowing that soon this place would be gone from my life forever.

Despite my father's ambivalence about the opulent world at the Park Lane, he rationalized his presence by making connections with the workers. He claimed that they respected him because he "fought for the working class." Maybe that was true. But he was married into the Park Lane family and benefitted from it in many ways, not the least of which was financial.

Mealtime is one of the binding structures of our lives, and this is even more pronounced in institutions like assisted living.

When my father moved into Harmony Village, he experienced a different kind of family restaurant than the Park Lane. It was not an elegant affair, but it was a respectable dining experience. First there was the procession of blue-haired elderly residents who stood outside the dining room, some in wheelchairs and some in walkers, waiting for the doors to officially open. Then there were the three mealtime shifts, regulated by rigid adherence to a schedule so the dining room would never become too crowded.

Whenever the doors opened, eager residents made a slow-moving, yet mad scramble to find a seat with their friends. Those who were visually impaired like my father didn't have much of a choice about where to sit, unless a family member or private caregiver led the way. At his most disgruntled, my father would gripe, "All people do in this place is eat." He maintained a gruff, dismissive emphasis on the phrase, "this place."

When I was caring for Red at Harmony Village, I liked to sit at a table with one of two couples. One of the couples—Bones and Lilly—met as residents. Bones was easily ten years older than Lilly. He was a trombone player who performed at the Park Lane in its hey-day, more than sixty years earlier. Red and Bones might have even been in the same room back then, with Bones playing music and my father, the husband of the hoity-toity restaurant owner, drinking his martini and eating his hors d'oeuvres, steak, potatoes, salad, and dessert. At Harmony Village, these two men found common ground. They were equals, connected by strands of their histories, which they could call upon, free of the details, to link past to present. It was safer that way.

Like the food at the Park Lane, the food at Harmony Village was considered one of its selling points. Nary a lobster dainty would you find. Harmony Village had traditional fare, 1950's style, without any flourish or spice. No salt and easy to chew. Making institutional food appealing is challenging enough, but accommodating the lowest common denominator—decaying teeth, rumbling guts, and fading taste buds—removes many options. By the time my father moved into Harmony Village, he had become a conscientiously healthy eater. Their menu wasn't up to snuff, but he never complained.

Living alone as my father did for more than twenty years is hard for any elderly eater, especially a man who never cooked for himself. He learned to prepare basic meals, some quite strange. When I suggested that he try tofu, he put chunks of raw tofu in his breakfast cereal to augment his protein intake and claimed it tasted good. He adjusted his diet to include easy-to-cook whole baked potatoes, with raw vegetables and fruits. Sometimes he ate out at the local Greek restaurant and lived on the leftovers for days. This was a step up from one of his brothers, an accountant all his life who managed to save until he amassed a fortune but still ate every meal at Denny's. Like my father, my uncle erred on the side of consistency: they knew him there, and it was reliable.

Mealtime at Harmony Village, as all residents quickly discovered, was hit-or-miss. While the fish fry on Friday nights was delicious, the lasagna could be overcooked and tasteless, and the vegetables were generally overcooked. Food fueled many a conversation among the residents. They welcomed a universal topic that would give them a sense of community. Simple chatter such as—"Did you try the soup today? Yes, it was quite good"—broke down a sense of isolation.

When my father was living in his home, he put a big sign on his fridge saying "EAT LESS," as he was persistently and unnecessarily worried about his weight. He got on a scale every morning, and if he had gained a pound, he would restrict his food intake that day. When he moved into Harmony Village, he had no choice but to relinquish some control and loosen his constraining standards. He might enjoy a small scoop of vanilla or chocolate ice cream, sometimes topped with runny chocolate syrup, maybe even with a piece of apple pie. He even resumed his coffee drinking habit after a forty-year hiatus. When I asked him about the coffee, he replied nonchalantly, "Oh, I enjoy drinking coffee these days," as if he hadn't missed a beat. At that moment, I felt a small shift in him. He was starting to find a rhythm as a resident at Harmony Village.

One of my favorite things about mealtime at Harmony Village was the staff, especially the young waif of a waitress named Geena. She looked like she had a hard-luck story of her own with her vulnerable mouth and sad eyes. To take orders, she would stoop down in front of each resident so they could see one another eye to eye. She would say their name and ask gently, "What are you going to have today?" She acted like she had no better place to be than right there, attentively guiding each person through the short menu with large type as they decided between lasagna and chicken with a side of green beans.

Rhoda's Paintings at Harmony Village

Every other weekend at Harmony Village, I felt trapped inside my father's tiny apartment, a veritable oasis in an institutional setting that he and I both found alien. It only took stepping out of the room to feel the sterility of the environment, despite the staff's efforts to make it feel as much like home as possible. Some residents tried to make it homey by decorating their doors with wreaths or a store-bought welcome sign, or by putting little tables outside their rooms covered with "tchotchkes" or trinkets. But the surrounding walls of the apartments were blank. It struck me that one way to broaden my father's world—and brighten the place for everyone—would be to hang some of my mother's paintings in the hallway outside of his apartment.

My mother was a prolific painter. Besides the workers at the Park Lane, she painted strangers from the Salvation Army who modeled for her classes and friends and relatives she could cajole into sitting for a portrait. In addition to the five or so portraits she did of me, she painted at least the same number of my sister, capturing different stages of our lives. She did a few portraits of my father, too, and self-portraits from her forties, fifties, and sixties, each looking progressively more morose. By the end of her life, my mother left behind unfinished portraits, overworked portraits, and a few random still-life paintings that had no life (see photo gallery). There are a few landscapes she painted when she was travelling to Boston Hills, a rural area outside of Buffalo, with a painter friend named Ruth. These paintings are loose and joyful, reflecting the pleasure she took in those languid, peaceful afternoons she spent with her friend creating watercolor landscapes amidst rolling hills and colorful vegetation. I felt that some of her more lively paintings would give the walls at Harmony Village a much-needed boost. But I wasn't sure what, if anything, would be allowed on the walls.

If we mounted some of my mother's paintings, it could also open the floodgates to others who had special pictures or portraits they wanted to hang, until the whole village might end up looking like a haphazard mural. But when I checked with the main nurse who seemed to make all the decisions at the village, she immediately said, "Yes! Bring them in!" Buoyed by her response, I burst into my father's room and announced exuberantly that we could create a little gallery outside of his room with my mother's paintings. But he flatly refused. No explanation. Just an adamant, "No!"

I'm not sure what I was expecting, exactly. I guess I hoped, and blissfully anticipated, that he would share my excitement in making this facility feel more like home. I was wrong. He didn't want his life at Harmony Village to extend beyond his room. This institution wasn't his home, and he didn't want to be there. Maybe he also felt too exposed having his wife's art publicly displayed. My best guess is that he wasn't ready to formalize his membership in the land of assisted living.

There was no point in trying to make my father change his mind. But several months later, he totally forgot about his adamant refusal and told me he wanted to display Rhoda's paintings in the hallways. I believe he was feeling grateful for the care provided to him at Harmony Village. But, by the time he wanted her paintings in the hallway outside of his room, we were focused on caring for him.

A Letter from Einstein

One great thing about assisted living is that residents can bring their own "stuff"; one bad thing is that the stuff needs to be winnowed down to the basics. My father's apartment at Harmony Village was a small L-shaped room. The first leg of the L was the living/dining/kitchen area. The bedroom was the perpendicular other half, with the bed taking up two-thirds of that space. Without much room left, residents needed to be choosey about what really counted when they moved in. Was it a bed or furniture or paintings or a TV? Was it a special chair or photographs?

For my father, the most important thing was the kitchen table. This is where he ate and talked on the phone and, in the past, had written letters and essays and plays. We had always called it "command central." It was a place where he felt a semblance of control and where he spent 75 percent of his time while living at Harmony Village. He even napped in front of his command central table, seated in a hard, straight-backed chair, another relic from his previous life, cherished for its familiarity. But even when a person's personal space holds recognizable cues—whether it's furniture or photographs or trinkets—it's still jarring to be away from one's own home.

Moreover, when life loses its familiar punctuations, the passage of time may lose its anchor. Knowing the day and time provides an orienting solace as people lose a grip on the everyday signposts. Over time, my father increasingly asked for this information because his vision had profoundly declined. Since we weren't always there to answer, we bought him a clock to do the job on demand. It was simple. Every time he pressed an easy-to-find button, a digital male voice announced said information in a confident, but stilted, tone. "Friday, 10 a.m.," the disassociated voice would declare. And my father would momentarily relax. But toward the end of his life, as his memory failed and anxiety increased, the frequency of button-pushing escalated. "Friday, 10 a.m., Friday, 10:01 a.m., Friday, 10:02 a.m.," until the voice created an absurd cacophony of announcements. It was painfully sad and more than I could bear.

Accumulated mail also piled up on the command central table, waiting for the arrival of my sister or me to review it with him. This ritual brought back the familiar, reminding our father of friends who sent notes we could savor, and that annoying junk mail we could jointly grouse about. The bills were set aside, saved for my sister, the elder. She was the executor of our father's estate. There was no point mentioning the bills to him when they arrived. It only conjured up worry.

On the wall opposite command central hung a framed portrait of my grandmother, his mother, who lived to be nearly one hundred years old. My mother had painted it approximately six decades earlier (see photo gallery). Even in old age, thoughts of one's mother can offer comfort. The only time I remember seeing my father cry was at his mother's funeral, as we were walking away from the gravesite.

Under the painting of my grandmother was a flat-screen television purchased by my brother-in-law, a tech-whiz. It was permanently set to CNN, the one channel that could produce news 24/7, even if it was a repetitive recycle of the same stories. The constant feed was apt for a news junkie with compromised eyesight and a failing memory that made channel surfing a burden. For a man who read up to ten papers per day and boasted encyclopedic knowledge about world affairs, the drone of nonstop news on CNN offered a strange sense of calm.

Above command central was another important link to my father's past, a letter from Albert Einstein dated April 16, 1954. My father explained in his autobiography that this letter was a response to one he had written to Einstein about an ethical matter involving the Fifth Amendment of the United States Constitution. When he was first subpoenaed to testify before the House Un-American Activities Committee in 1954, my father was deeply troubled about how to respond to the accusatory questions. Many witnesses cited the Fifth Amendment as their rebuttal, saying, "I refuse to answer the question on the grounds that I may incriminate myself." Witnesses did this as an act of protest and as a strategy to ward off invasive surveillance of their lives and the lives of others. My father respected their decision to use this strategy, but it didn't feel right to him. He was inspired by Einstein, who at the time was publicly encouraging witnesses to refuse to testify.

In a letter Albert Einstein wrote to Rose Russell, a member of the New York City Teachers Union, he argued that the Fifth Amendment did not offer "legal middle ground for [the person] to defend his actual rights." He maintained that "there is no other way other than revolutionary non-cooperation, like Gandhi used with great success against the legal powers of the British Authorities." This conclusion resonated with my father, who ultimately decided not to plead the Fifth Amendment. Following Einstein's lead, he challenged the constitutionality of the committee.

"I feel very indebted to you," Manny wrote to Einstein, "because your position regarding what witnesses should do when called before the [House Un-American Activities] committee had a great influence in helping me make my own decision" (see photo gallery).

What chutzpah for my father to write a letter like that to this esteemed scientist! To this day, I am proud that he chose this course and cannot imagine him taking any other.

Einstein's response to my father's letter was simple and concise, reflecting an implicit knowledge that his affirmation mattered. He told my father he "did the right thing."

> Dear Mr. Fried:
> I am convinced that you did the right thing and fulfilled
> your duty as a citizen *under difficult circumstances.*
> My respect, Albert Einstein

Einstein's letter was typewritten except for the words "under difficult circumstances." These were handwritten by Einstein, ostensibly as an afterthought but, nonetheless, a recognition—almost an understatement—of the horrendous circumstances my father endured. Einstein approved of my father's decision to challenge the right of HUAC to exist, making the strong statement that what the committee was doing was wrong. Einstein's support of my father's controversial actions is not surprising, given his own position in relation to HUAC and his own firsthand experience with the FBI, which kept a dossier on him for more than twenty years. What is remarkable about this letter is that Einstein took the time to write it.

When my father wrote his infamous letter to Einstein, he made an interesting statement. He said, "I think you will be glad to hear that the position you took has received a good response from the many working people I am in constant contact with. I myself have received the most wonderful kind of expressions of support from our union members since I refused to answer any of the questions of the committee and challenged its very right to exist."

I am struck by two things in this passage. Perhaps the most apparent is that my father presumes that Einstein, a top scientist at Princeton University, might not have been aware of the ramifications of his positions regarding HUAC among working-class people. My father wrote to him as an emissary from another world to say, you, Einstein, have a following among MY people.

I'm also struck by my father's acknowledgement that he had received "the most wonderful kind of expressions of support from our union members." As his daughter, my impression was that he was overwhelmingly isolated and alone during this period. But this letter confirms to me that he was not alone among his union buddies. Yes, he was alone in relation to my mother, who saw her world crumbling as a result of her husband's stance as an outspoken labor leader and activist. It was in her world—the world of upper-class Jews, a rarified "class" of people who barely counted as upper class because they were Jews—where this Jewish working-class hero was perceived as a threat to the social ladder they were climbing. In this context, as my father struggled for affirmation, a letter from Albert Einstein would mean a great deal.

My father displayed a copy of the Einstein letter in his assisted living apartment until his death, four days shy of age ninety-eight, with the original letter securely stored in a locked security box at the local M&T Bank in Buffalo.

Aging and Cumulative Loss

When my father first arrived at Harmony Village, his body was weakened by the failure of three major organs—heart, lung, and kidneys—which sapped his physical energy and muted his character. Oxygen was ordered for him initially just to aid physical movement, but over the next several months, it had to be increased until it was on 24/7. In his small living room sat the "mother ship" of oxygen, a bulky white plastic lifeline planted against the wall, fixed to a tentacle that transported the colorless, odorless gas into my father's nose. Every time he went to the bathroom, which was frequent, he needed to be untethered to avoid tripping over the plastic tubing as he gingerly made the seven or so steps to the toilet. Every time he lumbered back to his chair and plopped down with effort, the tube was reinserted into his nose, a permanent but necessary discomfort.

Whenever my father left the room, he had to use a portable system of oxygen-filled canisters, which weighed about seven pounds. The nurses schooled us on how to turn the canisters on and off and how to change them when the oxygen was too low. We had to monitor the pressure gauge and turn the knob in the correct direction to release the oxygen, and the tank began to feel very heavy if we carried it for any length of time. Those bullet-like vessels terrified me. If a tank were to fall over, it could break and the oxygen could escape, an extremely dangerous situation. Given the emotionally high stakes, for me, dealing with them was torture.

Every morning, an aide would come into my father's room to wake him and dress him for the day. Before he could leave for breakfast, he was weighed to make sure he wasn't retaining too much fluid, a marker of his diseased heart. The running record—165, 168, 174 pounds—was maintained on a chart to the left of the tiny bathroom sink, a constant reminder of the precariousness of his health. Three times a day, another nurse would come in and administer a series of eye medications for macular degeneration, a disease that accounts for 60 percent of all vision disorders in older adults. In the last year of his life, this degenerative condition robbed my father of his vision, just as it had done to his brother Maurie.

I still think about my father's blue, piercing eyes, and how he communicated through them, channeling his anger, his passion, his compassion, his vulnerability—eyes that became cloudy and distant. Just another indicator of loss. At the very least, his eye medications kept his eyes pain-free and supposedly slowed down the deterioration of his eyesight.

Although at times my father still looked at me as we talked, he increasingly stared ahead. I would wonder what he was thinking, whether he was becoming more internal or just fading away. A character in Dante's *Divine Comedy* says, "The eyes here are the windows of the soul." Even if the window was too cloudy to see through, I believed he was still in there somewhere. I found ways to adapt, making connections through other means, like voice and touch. Sometimes I played music for him, and he'd smile and sing along. And he always relaxed when I massaged his neck and shoulders, afterward thanking me quietly. I wasn't ready to let go, and neither was he.

In the 1990s, I conducted a study with sociologist Claire Reinelt in which we explored the experiences of mothers with disabilities (Fried and Reinelt 1998). The range of disabilities among the mothers we interviewed included multiple sclerosis, visual impairment, and cerebral palsy. We wanted to know how these mothers coped with the challenges of parenting. How did they negotiate the division of labor with their partners? Were their children different from kids of parents without disabilities?

We discovered that mothers who lived for years with a disability were adept at finding creative adaptations to live life fully, including embracing the challenging task of mothering young children. These mothers tended to share care more equally with their partners because that, too, was necessary and adaptive. Because their children had grown up with a parent with a disability, it was the norm rather than something unusual. The problems the mothers faced had less to do with their disability and more to do with society's negative perspectives on disability. A great example was the mom who was downtown with her four-year-old boy and needed directions. When she asked a stranger on the street for help, he directed the response to her four-year-old, instead of to the child's visually impaired mother.

The longer we live—and we are living a lot longer than we did a few decades ago—the more likely we will eventually experience loss of some function or other. Unlike the people in our study who had lifelong disabilities, these later-arrival disabilities are not something for which we have time to adapt. A lot of us dread these losses and perhaps demonstrate less creativity in adapting to them compared to the person for whom it is the norm. An activist with severe cerebral palsy told me years ago, with a touch of humor, "We call you people TABBIES, temporarily able-bodied." While I understood what she was saying intellectually, it has taken me many years—and my own process of aging—to more fully comprehend that we may be "able-bodied" when we are younger, but as we age, we all experience diminished functioning. A certain amount of loss is part of the trajectory of life.

For my father, hearing loss was slow and progressive. By the time he reached ninety, his capacity to follow a conversation in a large group setting was significantly compromised. In contrast, a serious highway accident resulted in an abrupt change in his health, a life-threatening cervical spine injury which required surgery and a difficult recuperation period. But my father believed that if he exercised hard and stayed involved with his intellectual life, he could forestall the wear and tear of aging. He even claimed that he was still running at age eighty-five, even though, as I clearly recall, his run had become a crawl combined with a slow walk. But maintaining his routine and belief that he was in control did serve him. It kept him in the world of the familiar where he could wave to the same group of fellow runners and walkers in Buffalo's Delaware Park. He was part of the fabric of his community.

Through research, now popularized in mass media, we know that maintaining good nutrition and consistent exercise goes a long way toward staying physically strong and mentally alert, sometimes preventing all kinds of terrible diseases, including heart disease, stroke, hypertension, anxiety, depression, obesity, and osteoporosis. The pathway of cumulative loss may be far more affected by lifestyle and access to quality medical care than genetics. But loss doesn't necessarily happen overnight. It can be a slow and incremental process.

By the time someone lands in an assisted living facility, she or he has experienced cumulative loss, both physical and emotional, often having suffered the death of significant others, perhaps including spouses, relatives, and good friends. Still it came as a shock when we learned that our father was living with his trio of organ failures. My vision of him as old but hearty had clouded my ability to recognize the severity of his condition.

Watching a parent dissolve in front of you is devastating. But with each new level of loss, I adjusted, grieving each one of them one by one—the eyes, the hearing, the ambulation, the heart, the lungs, the mind. I felt an increased responsibility to be a responsible daughter, to provide him with support and comfort, and to advocate for him wherever he was, in assisted living or at the hospital or in a rehab facility. To do it "right" became my job. I had to learn about each new disease he faced and figure out ways—sometimes obvious, sometimes nuanced—to support him so that he could maintain his sense of dignity and independence to the greatest extent possible. Despite my sadness, I took pleasure in that.

Weight Lifting with Lorna

The daily routine at Harmony Village was predictable. Residents were assigned to one of three mealtime slots that punctuated the day. In between meals, various activities were offered, such as crafts, games, and movies, and there were two exercise classes per day, one in the morning and one in the afternoon. Often a Friday night included a very popular happy hour, with watered-down alcoholic drinks in small paper cups and munchies like chips and dip. Occasionally in the evenings, a local musician, either an accordionist or pianist, came by for an hour to perform "oldies." On Sunday mornings, a subset of the same group gathered to be driven to church, first sitting or standing in the hallway waiting for the van, and then returning an hour and a half later.

Holiday parties were peppered into the Harmony Village schedule. During the Christmas season, the facility was decorated with sparkling lights and a large tree. A life-size, rotund Santa Claus stood in the front hallway, waving his electrically generated hand as people entered the facility, and an empty menorah sat nearby, a small nod to Chanukah and the less obvious Jewish population at Harmony Village. In the spring, Easter decorations were ubiquitous, lending a more festive feel to the institution. Special meals during those occasions were consistently counted on and appreciated as well.

So it went with the routines of Harmony Village, potentially dull, but consistent by design, intended to foster a sense of calm and order for residents in their new, and often, final home.

Before breakfast, an aide was assigned to come to my father's room to wake him up and help him dress. His favorite aide was Janelle, and it was no wonder. She was warm and attentive, a Jamaican woman with a lilting voice who had mastered the fine art of providing respectful support to frail elders on tasks that could otherwise have been construed as humiliating, like bathing, changing adult diapers, and helping with toileting. Sadly, after a few months, Janelle was moved to another floor, a decision that was out of her control. She grumbled to me about it, and I complained to her supervisor, to no avail. I was told that these decisions are complicated and not made lightly, and I was reminded that this was a place in which everyone's needs must be balanced and to some degree, met.

It was clear that the next aide was not nearly as artful in her handling of my father, but worse, she turned out to be thoughtless and inept. At one point, my father told me that she had refused to pick up his hearing aid when it dropped to the floor, chiding him by saying, "You can do that yourself," as she walked away. He was outraged, but didn't have the energy, or the words for that matter, to protest. That role had been transferred to me. I complained bitterly to my favorite nurse about the aide's unacceptable behavior, and I assumed it stopped, because I didn't hear any more complaints from my father. Then I discovered that the aide wasn't getting to my father's room in time to help him dress for breakfast, which meant that he wasn't eating in the morning. Again, I complained, and finally, another aide was assigned to the floor.

The job of caregiver requires vigilance in uncovering problems and diplomacy in confronting those in charge. I was very careful to treat the nursing staff and aides with due respect. Although I believe they sought to provide high-quality care to all residents, their attention, by virtue of the nature of the job, was pulled in multiple directions, which meant they had to prioritize those who were most in need. More than once, people told me that "the squeaky wheel gets the grease." But, if you complain too much, there's always the risk of a backlash—being viewed as the ungrateful, demanding daughter. This was tricky terrain to negotiate. Ultimately, my goal was to find a balance, to get my father's needs met while respecting the workers and the needs of other residents.

My father developed renal failure, so he took medication to control elimination and had to be weighed daily to make sure he wasn't retaining water. Later, the nurse would review his numbers and adjust his medications accordingly. His health was precarious. With congenital heart failure, excessive water retention can be lethal. The two organs, I discovered—the kidneys and the heart—are linked. I learned something new every day about things I never needed to know, until then.

The journey to breakfast was a chore unto itself. Like clockwork, the doors from apartments along the hallway opened, and a slow cavalcade of residents groaned toward the elevator, which took them down to the dining hall. The early birds avoided the big rush; they were willing to wait outside the dining room so they could get first dibs on their favorite table. But those unwilling or unable to get out of their apartments any earlier might find a jam-up at the elevator, where a convocation of residents using wheelchairs, walkers, and canes made their first public appearance of the day.

After breakfast, some people dallied and chatted in the dining room; others slowly faded out of the room and returned to their apartments where they rested, watched television, or read. Elevator notices reminded residents of the activity schedule with a daily flyer that advertised "Word Games with Ellen" or "Mojito Happy Hour" or "Weight Class with Lorna." There was no dearth of fun in this place, I gathered. Some residents were visited by roving nurses who pushed heavy medication carts several times a day as they made their rounds. But the next real event was lunch, followed by more optional activities, and then dinner. When he first arrived at Harmony Village, my father scorned bingo. He hissed at me, "These people! We have nothing in common!" Bingo became a larger-than-life symbol of why he felt he did not belong there. Underlying his disdain for bingo and the people who played it was his fear that he was or might become like "them." Aside from his snobbishness, he was also incredibly shy, and didn't really know how to break into conversation that wasn't framed by discussion of theater, politics, or his own accomplishments.

One time when my sister was visiting, he said, "You know how to talk with people." He admired her ability to make chit-chat with strangers in the dining room at Harmony Village, telling her that he didn't feel comfortable doing that. She countered, saying he just had to talk to people about what's important to them in their lives, like their children or where they used to live. But he resisted, remaining quiet-spoken and hesitant to plunge into a new social world with what he saw as an alien set of people. He had always resisted being part of an age-defined culture of elders, and what he really had in common with this particular group was the reality that this was likely their last home, and without question, their final chapter.

In the 1960s, two experts on aging, Elaine Cumming and William Henry (1961), posited that it was normal for older people to increasingly withdraw from interaction with others around them as they approached the end of their lives. Aging, they argued, inevitably involved the dissolution of social roles, such as one's identity as a worker or active community member. Ultimately, they said, elders naturally deteriorated and grew more isolated. The inevitability of disengagement was fiercely critiqued, as other aging experts argued that it was not a given. Gerontologist Robert Atchley (1989) argued that, rather than disengaging from society, middle-aged and older adults made deliberate choices to stay involved in activities that called upon past experiences, skills, and interests. Moreover, he argued, one's internal structure—an individual's psyche and even his or her personality—remains constant throughout life and into old age. According to this theory of *continuity*, adult development is a continuous process, in which we can—and should—continue to fuel the interests and passions of our younger years. Perhaps our ability to dance or play the flute or knit may diminish, but our enjoyment and appreciation of these activities do not change. Continuity theory challenges the orthodoxy that people become unproductive and useless as they grow older.

My father was always an athlete. He got into college on a football scholarship, one he unfortunately lost because he wasn't good enough, or so he said. Later, when he was in New York pursuing an acting career, he claimed he had danced with the modern dance great, Martha Graham, something I found hard to believe because, despite his athleticism, he was clumsy! Every morning of my growing-up years, he grunted through a harsh set of exercises that he had learned in the army, which involved a quantum number of full-body push-ups, a gaggle of sit-ups, but none of the stretching we now know is equally important to keep our muscles supple and strong. Even when it wasn't cool to be a runner—back in the 1960s—my father would "run" our dog, Charlie, for a mile or more. It was considered quirky and somewhat endearing by a number of our neighbors who still remember those morning runs.

Throughout my young adult years, my father and I did three-mile runs together. As I now calculate his age at that point, I realize that we were running together until he was well into his seventies.

During one visit, in which we all converged at my aunt and uncle's house in Swampscott, a coastal town north of Boston, my father and I disappeared for a four-hour walk. We were so engaged in chatting that we totally forgot about time and location, and we got utterly lost. Eventually, we found our way back to familiar landmarks, unfazed by circuitous wanderings along winding roads. When we finally sauntered happily into the house, my mother was furious at me, lashing at me with spitting blame, "You're going to kill him!" He and I didn't take her seriously and just laughed off her anger. I knew he was okay because I observed his strength and endurance. But I was also complicit in the passive-aggressive ways in which he discounted her.

The only casualties were the few blisters on his feet because he walked for four hours in dress shoes! Even then, he had the stamina and strength to push the limits. We now know, of course, from plenty of research on the effects of exercise on aging, that his sustained exercise routines probably contributed to the quality and length of his long life.

Aside from mealtime, one of the most popular activities at Harmony Village was Lorna's free-weights exercise class. Although nurses were the ubiquitous presence at the facility, Lorna was its heart and soul. Effervescent and loving, she roamed the halls, enticing residents to join her for class. "Just ten minutes, Fiona! I hope I'll see you there!" Often Lorna's eight-year-old daughter accompanied her. The girl's best friend there was a ninety-year-old woman who wore a bevy of outrageously colorful and oversized hats graced with feathers and ribbons. Lorna often got things rolling with balloon volleyball, a game I associated with young children, but at Harmony Village, it seemed like an ageless amusement. It was pretty straightforward. She stood in the middle of the circle of residents, who were all seated in their chairs or wheelchairs, and flipped the balloon around the room, making sure everyone had a turn. Some were very cautious with it; others gave it a big whack and laughed out loud. The sound of their joy was delicious.

My father, who was legally blind, anticipated the balloon coming his way, with his hand ready to give the balloon a pop. When it came into his line of vision and nearly hit him, his hand remarkably made contact with the ball, and it ricocheted back into the circle. He was self-amused and smiled wanly, a simple response that warmed my heart and let me know that he was still "in there." There were fewer and fewer of those moments. A frail woman sat next to him, body rigid, eyes blank, seemingly unaware that this game was happening in her midst. But when the ball came toward her, Lorna screamed her name, and she woke up just in time and gave it a gentle ping, barely saving it from floating down in front of her.

I was amazed at how long the group enjoyed playing this game. Even though the class was called weight exercise, this weightless balloon volleyball game constituted about three-quarters of our time. I joined in, mixing up my "moves" with moderately hard punches and an occasional soccer head hit, which elicited titters from the crowd. Later in the dining hall, when I saw some of my balloon volleyball teammates, they smiled at me, and I felt more connected to this place.

All of the fun and games were punctuated by an undercurrent of failing health, as residents noticed who was not showing up at Lorna's exercise class or at bingo, or as someone was rushed out of the building on a stretcher. When we sat down for lunch one day with Bones, the musician who had once played at the Park Lane, he whispered to me, "How is Mack doing?" Bones's girlfriend, Lilly, reminded him that my father's name wasn't Mack, and said chidingly, "You've got it wrong again!" a touch of annoyance she sprinkled with a slice of humor. Bones said to me hopefully, "Mack looks really good, just the same as when he first moved in, doesn't he?" ignoring Lilly's correction. The fact was that "Mack" was not doing too well at all, but I didn't have the heart to tell Bones.

Over the year, my father gradually succumbed to bingo. In the beginning, he would smile at me as he said sardonically, "All anybody ever does here is gamble!" To him, bingo was a game that reeked of "old person," an insipid pastime for people who had nothing else to do with their lives. For a man of purpose, bingo was a waste of time, an indicator that one's important work was over, that life was now about biding time until you die. He also scoffed at bingo because he was not a "gambling man." But I recalled that, many years before when his traveling improvisational theater troupe had gone to Las

Vegas to perform, he "allowed" himself to play the slot machines, albeit for just $20 per day, coming out even at the end.

Later, I found out that he had started playing dice at Harmony Village with Paul, a friend who came to visit him every week. Paul was a fellow actor, a gruff but warm man who saw humor in everyday life. Paul told me that bingo was good for my father, and undoubtedly Paul got a charge out of it himself. But, first, the dice games began. I noticed that my father was stacking quarters daily, and Paul told me in a bemused tone, "Your father has been winning a lot lately!" Then came bingo. My father began to enter foreign territory, the world of old people, and despite himself, he managed to have fun.

If the first stage of my father's residency at Harmony Village was characterized by resistance to being identified with the institution, the next stage featured partial acquiescence, as he allowed himself to take advantage of certain aspects of the institution's culture. With the companionship of Paul, he was perhaps able to accept that he actually resided at Harmony Village and that he might as well have some unfettered fun while there.

Even though he began to play dice and bingo every day, he still insisted that he was not like "them." But his participation began to break down whatever prejudices he had against his fellow residents, and he reversed his position and said, "There are some good people here." It was understandable that he wouldn't want to get too invested in the people around him because sometime soon—perhaps in a few months or in a year or the next year—they would die. Even though he was joining in, he maintained his distance from this group of elders by making fun of their activities.

One day, my father and I were in the dining hall, eating our salads and waiting for the main course to come. The choice that day was chicken parmesan or chili, and he opted for the chicken "parm." He asked for a coffee, presumably to wake him up. Our friends, Bones and Lilly, sat two tables away, but still within earshot. When they saw us, Bones waved wildly and called across the room, "How's it going, Mack?" My father didn't reply, so I said, "He's doing fine." Bones smiled and waved again. I could see that he wished we were sitting together. I wished we were sitting together, too. Bones was a talker, and it was more interesting to sit with him and Lilly than to sit with my father alone, where I felt compelled to keep a running dialogue. This was, no doubt, my own "stuff," but I could not succumb to being another silent table of people who stare into space. It was just too depressing.

I realized that it was catch-as-catch-can as to whether my father would respond. Given his failing health and near-blindness, he didn't seem interested in conversing, nor did he care about being silent or about the meaning or appearance of his silence. I was his eyes and ears, watching to observe and to understand the world of this place. His former self would have been proselytizing about politics or story-telling about his theater or writing past. But at this point, he didn't seem to care. His behavior didn't appear strange to anyone there, though. There were many more like him, who quietly sat and supped.

Firing Dr. Fine

Over the year, my sister and I grew increasingly frustrated with Dr. Fine and tentatively began looking for a geriatrician, a medical doctor who specializes in treating older people. Increasingly, we questioned Dr. Fine's judgment. Our concerns began when he prescribed Ambien for our dad and they progressed because he seemed confused and forgetful, misplacing important documents and forgetting important pieces of information. Despite the fact that my father was devoted to Dr. Fine, we felt that it was in our father's best interests to switch practitioners. But firing a parent's doctor is no mean feat, especially when that parent doesn't want to make a change.

Dr. Fine should have retired years earlier, but my father didn't want to make the break. He trusted this doctor implicitly, claiming proudly that he was Dr. Fine's first patient, forty years ago. Dr. Fine knew my father as a vibrant and accomplished playwright, actor, and labor leader, and that was important to him. I understood my father's sentiment. Why wouldn't he want to stay with a practitioner who had watched and reveled in his full life?

As we grow older, our frailties become what are visible in the end stage of our lives, rather than the rich tapestry of our overall life trajectory. I'm sure my father feared that a new doctor would see only an old man stripped of his identity, a nobody, instead of an accomplished writer and activist who had suffered deeply and fought so hard to make his mark on the world. Unfortunately, my father's loyalty to Dr. Fine obscured his vision, making it difficult for him to recognize that he was receiving inferior care. He didn't seem to connect the dots. Even when my sister and I pleaded with him to switch doctors, enumerating the reasons why we questioned Dr. Fine's judgment, he calmly tried to reassure us. "Dr. Fine is an excellent doctor. And he cares a lot about me." Yes, he does, we would say, but that doesn't make him a good doctor.

I'm sure that his resistance to leaving Dr. Fine was also grounded in a basic fear of change, going from a known entity to an unknown one. There had been a lot of that kind of change already, starting with moving out of the house where he had lived for decades and into a facility that represented his final chapter of life. Keeping the same doctor may have felt like the anchor, even though that anchor was getting rusty. But fear of change couldn't be what held back his daughters from finding a high-quality practitioner. Ultimately, my sister and I stopped trying to understand our father's fears or rigidity, and we set up a visit for him to meet with a respected geriatrician. We reassured him that he didn't have to leave Dr. Fine, only that he needed to meet with the new doctor.

We also discovered, to our delight, that this geriatrician, whom everyone called Dr. Dave, made "house" visits at Harmony Village once a week. This meant that our father would not need to suffer through the increasingly arduous process of preparing for and leaving the building, of being driven to yet another appointment, of bearing the exhausting process of getting out of the car and walking into an office building, of finding a place to sit and rest before moving into the doctor's office and waiting to see the doctor, and finally, after being seen by the doctor, of reversing the entire process and returning home several hours later, thoroughly drained. Instead, Dr. Dave could see my father in the comfort of his own apartment for half an hour every week, timing his visit so that it fell conveniently between breakfast and the exercise class with Lorna.

And so, despite his initial resistance, he relented and agreed to meet Dr. Dave just to "check him out." To our delight, the doctor was an experienced practitioner committed to working with frail elders. He listened with a nuanced ear to our father, learned about his medical status, and more importantly, was able to see him as a full person with a past, present, and future. That evening, we caught up with the doctor to review this initial visit, and he told us, "I expected to see a very sick man, based on what I read in his medical charts and he is, but I also saw a vibrant and lucid man with a very interesting history." We sighed with relief.

Thankfully, our father responded in kind, saying that "this new, young doctor" seemed like a "nice guy who seems very knowledgeable." The key to our father's approval was the fact that Dr. Dave viewed him as the fully accomplished man that he was, not simply as a composite of his medical problems. After this first visit, my sister captured my sentiment completely, saying, "Dr. Dave is youthful and smart and seems to 'get him.'" Ultimately, Dr. Fine meant well, but that wasn't enough. Quietly and without any fanfare, my sister and I did the ultimate in taking charge: we fired Dr. Fine and hired Dr. Dave, and we were comforted to know that our father would be receiving quality medical care.

Remington Rand

From the time I was a little girl, my father told me stories about his experience as a union organizer. He never altered his language to make these stories easier to grasp. I don't think he really knew how to do that. His stories were impassioned diatribes about workers getting fed up with low wages and lousy working conditions. And more often than not, he was the hero of his tales, as he described leading a group of workers to protest some injustice. I learned that bosses are bad and workers are good. I learned that labor and management don't get along. I learned that some leaders of the Catholic Church had stood on the wrong side, fighting the union and, in specific, besmirching my father's name. It was a black and white world, with very little room for gray.

Although I rarely met the workers my father was organizing, I became familiar with phrases he used to describe their actions, like "going out on strike" or "walking out," or "negotiating with the bosses." He adamantly wanted me to listen and comprehend. I found these stories boring and repetitive and difficult to understand, but at the same time, I believed and trusted in him, and as always, assumed that he was right. Sometimes I just felt stupid because I thought I should be able to understand better, and sometimes the stories simply washed over me because the people and the circumstances didn't connect to anything in my day-to-day life as a child or as an adolescent. The basic tenet that came through was that you must stand up for your beliefs, no matter what.

Later, when I was in my teens and had felt the sting of being rejected by certain friends because of my father's political beliefs, the tenet began to sink in. I saw how my father had made some difficult choices, despite their consequences for our family. Maybe I had to believe his choices were the right ones; otherwise, I might have felt he didn't love us enough, putting his ideals before his family's needs and desires. Only when he turned ninety and began to examine the choices he had made did he give voice to any doubts that he had done the right thing. His situation was untenable, undeniably. But, if I had been in a similar circumstance, as a parent and a labor leader, would I have chosen the same route? As a young child, I didn't question. I simply looked up to him and admired the strength of his conviction.

Many years later, when I attended a conference of "red diaper babies," or children of parents who had been members of the Communist Party, I learned that the majority of the other "babies"—now adults who were trying to make sense of their past—had had two parents who shared the same leftist political beliefs. Their parents were organizers and teachers and postal workers and government workers who went to the same meetings; they invited friends who shared their beliefs into their homes to socialize and to organize; and they sent their children to the same "commie" summer camps, which reinforced the ideologies their children were taught in the home. I envied this consistency and apparent lack of tension in their homes. In contrast, my parents epitomized class conflict, two individuals—one working class, the other upper class—who inhabited disparate worlds. Their common ground was their art, and yet they struggled to find mutual friends. My mother, who loved cocktail parties, joked that she would place her guests' drinks on a tray from left to right, according to their political beliefs.

For many years, my image of working-class people was pretty hazy. There was Mike, a warm man with a raspy voice who always smiled when he saw me. He was the only working-class guy I can remember coming to the house, but I don't recall him sitting down for a coffee or a drink. There was always a quick delivery of a package, accompanied by a quiet chat with my father, and a fleeting smile at me on the way in and out of the house. Later, my father discovered that Mike may have been an informant for the FBI because he confessed in very general terms to my father that there were things he had done, things he could not discuss, for which he felt shame. Betrayal knew no class.

When I was in my twenties, I happened to share a row on a plane with a husky, middle-aged businessman who liked to chat. By that time, I had been involved in the Vietnam era anti-war movement and the second wave of the women's movement, and this man wasn't someone with whom I would normally engage. So I was curious. What is it about that suspended time spent with a stranger, tens of thousands of feet above the ground? Perhaps it is the anonymity of the relationship. Or a basic fear of flying that motivates strangers to use their potential last moment of connection to share the story of their lives. Or perhaps we talk in order to fend off sheer boredom, to make time pass quickly, or to experience adventure in a closed capsule where we hope that nothing will go horribly wrong.

In any case, we began to chat. And I learned that my new companion had been the owner of the Remington Rand factory at the same time that my father had organized its workers! A chill went through my body. In order to hear anything about his perspective on the parallel narrative I had been hearing my whole life from my father, I would have to maintain my secret as we spoke. So I played the role of the curious stranger, simply asking my seatmate about his work. In our hour or so of suspended time and space, he spoke openly about running the business and his frustration with his workers.

"I told them I was moving the factory abroad and offered them the opportunity to move with it," he told me. To his surprise, the workers didn't view this offer as an opportunity; rather, they wanted to stay where they were rooted with their families and friends. "They could have been adventurous," he declared. "Why were they being so childish?" *Childish*? I was appalled at his condescension. But I kept my thoughts to myself. As we spoke, I savored the fact that he had no idea whom he was talking to. I remembered my father's stories about trying to negotiate with him, and here he was, sitting right next to me on an airplane, clueless and obstinate. I quietly listened to his disgruntlement, and knowing that my father had organized his workers made me feel proud. I had encountered "the enemy" and survived undetected.

4

Bringing Vibrancy into the Last Stage of Life

When Assisted Living Is Not Enough

I believe strongly that all residents in assisted living facilities must be treated with dignity and that their privacy and autonomy should be respected. I cannot imagine putting my father into a facility where this was not the case. But here's the challenge for those of us who are adult children of frail elders. You cannot be there all the time, and your adult parents may not be able to communicate small or even larger infractions. Moreover, because the move to this new home can be traumatizing, representing a loss of autonomy and control, the feedback elders provide their children may be skewed or nonexistent. Although my sister and I knew that assisted living was the best option for our father once he could no longer safely remain in his own home, we did not anticipate the limitations of assisted living, nor how we would accommodate or work around them.

Like many residents in assisted living or any out-of-home facility, my father, as I've mentioned, initially didn't want to be there. No matter how caring or welcoming the employees were, he felt like a fish out of water, and I'm not surprised. I bet that many other residents felt the same way. Ultimately, I felt that, as his daughters, we needed to be vigilant in monitoring the care he received when we were onsite, we needed to be there as much as possible, and we needed "proxies" to let us know how he was doing. Those proxies could be trusted individuals within the institution, or they could be friends who visited throughout the week. But we needed "eyes and ears" that represented our father's interests.

Despite my worries, within a month or so, my sister and I had relaxed because we could see that our father was being cared for very well, even if he remained resistant to settling in at Harmony Village. The amalgam of employees was, overall, caring and thorough, and there seemed to be a staff-wide approach to interacting with residents that contributed to a culture of care that was warm and professional at the same time. I was grateful for Lorna, the activities coordinator, who cheerfully roamed the halls trying to seduce residents into her classes, and then treated each and every resident like they were a member of her family. The nurses were efficient, professional, and kind; and the aides seemed respectful and easy-going with residents. The dining room waitstaff were downright pleasant; the head of food services was absolutely jolly. Even the fix-it guy was kind and charming, and seemed remarkably skilled.

According to the National Center on Assisted Living (NCAL 2014), services should address not only residents' physical needs but also their emotional, intellectual, social, and spiritual well-being. That is a huge responsibility, and at Harmony Village, we felt that the staff aimed to achieve all of that. Bottom line, we had no fears of abuse or neglect, nor did we worry that a complaint would engender reprisal, two important factors raised by NCAL's guiding principles for achieving quality programming in assisted living. Harmony Village proudly asserts that it is a "warm and welcoming community" and promises to provide trained and caring staff twenty-four hours a day to assist with basic activities of daily living. But there came a point where assisted living wasn't enough, although it took a while to discover what was not in their purview.

When our father entered Harmony Village, we looked at the menu of services offered. Initially, we focused on the room options, which included one- and two-bedroom apartments, each with a different price tag. We selected a single, because that was what we could afford and it was sufficient, given his needs. In addition to a private living space, there were common spaces that were open to all residents, including the library and various activity rooms. The baseline menu also included three meals per day, provided in the dining room, and a panoply of activities such as exercise classes, regular bingo and card games, happy hours on Fridays, the occasional entertainer who tended to play "oldies" on an accordion or guitar, and afternoon and evening movies. Also, free van service was available for weekly shopping expeditions and other outside field trips. Beyond these offerings, the menu was a la carte, and for each additional set of services, there was an additional fee.

Studies by groups like the National Center on Assisted Living, the Center for Disease Control (CDC), and the Assisted Living Federation of America (ALFA), reveal that residents in assisted living need help with an average of 4.5 activities of daily living.[1] Eighty percent need help with housework, laundry, medications, transportation, and meal preparation. Break these numbers down, and they look like this: Nearly three-quarters of residents need help with bathing, compared to nearly all residents in nursing homes. Slightly over fifty percent need help with dressing, compared to 90 percent of residents in nursing homes. About one-third of assisted living residents need help with toileting, compared with 84 percent of residents in nursing homes. And more than four-fifths of assisted living residents need help with their medications, averaging about ten per day, including more than seven prescription drugs and more than two over-the-counter medications.

At Harmony Village, we "topped up" our basic services with additional care. For example, we paid to have an aide come into our father's room to give him regular baths and help him dress in the mornings. We also paid for a nurse to come to his room to administer medications three times per day, because he no longer could self-administer his eye drops for macular degeneration.

According to researchers Ethel Mitty (2003), Heather Young (2008), and others, many assisted living facilities play a role in medication management, either providing these services themselves or contracting with another home care provider to do so. In fact, Mitty says that between 50 and 75 percent of assisted living residents receive some help with managing their medication. However, they say that more often staff at these facilities monitor residents' medications but do not dispense them.

Young argues that monitoring the safety of medication management in assisted living can be more complex than in skilled nursing facilities because, in the former case, residents are mobile. Unlike in nursing homes, which function as single repositories for medication dispersal and monitoring, residents in assisted living may use multiple pharmacies, so for those assisted living facilities that DO offer medication management, coordination is critical to ensuring that residents are getting the correct medications on the right schedules.

Around fourteen states require that licensed nurses administer medications in assisted living facilities. However, some researchers point out that some facilities allow unlicensed staff to deliver and monitor meds and that the staff often lack adequate training regarding medication side effects, drug interactions, and safe delivery methods. Unfortunately, no recognized "safety standard" regulates how medication is managed in assisted living. As caregivers, if we are in the process of finding an assisted living facility, it's important to find out if and how medication is managed. And if our loved one is already in an assisted living facility, we can still monitor how medication is being dispensed and monitored.

When we first looked at Harmony Village, we didn't have the language, much less the understanding that we should be asking about the provision of this important service. As it turned out, we were very lucky that Harmony Village had the capacity to dispense and monitor medications, and an excellent nursing staff to do the job well. But we soon discovered that much of what our father needed wasn't covered in the basic cost of care. The more care he needed, the more we paid. Medication management, just like dressing and bathing, were add-ons to the basic services offered at Harmony Village.

When my father was about eighty years old, he purchased a long-term care policy, which, after an enormous amount of wrangling on our part, paid for all of this care. When I say "an enormous amount of wrangling," I mean weekly calls to the insurance company followed by a string of e-mails documenting our conversations, followed by more phone calls and a lot of waiting to find out whether the services that fell under our policy would actually be covered. Add to that a talkative worker who claimed that the one fax machine in the office wasn't working, and we were ready to climb a wall!

Whether it was really worth it for him to pay for long-term care insurance at his late age is questionable, since to get his "money's worth," he would have had to live at least a few more years. At the same time, it gave us a sense of comfort to have a chunk of money dedicated to paying for the multiple levels of services he ultimately required.

Long-term care insurance is the largest out-of-pocket expense for most elderly individuals. Approximately seven to nine million Americans—or 11 percent of the population of those fifty-five and over—currently have this type of insurance. Like my sister and me, most people are overwhelmed as they try to figure out the pros and cons of whether to purchase it. The costs of long-term care insurance varies tremendously, and from 2014 to 2015, the cost increased by 8.9 percent (American Association for Long-Term Care Insurance 2015). Long-term care insurance is more likely to be used—and cheaper—if it's purchased earlier in life. I'm sure my father didn't know this when he purchased his policy. Not surprisingly, women's premiums are higher than men's because women, in the aggregate, live longer.

According to economist Jeffrey Brown (2011), there are a number of barriers to purchasing long-term care insurance. Many people don't know how the program works, and they don't trust that it will pay out when they need it. Given this distrust, they may choose not to purchase long-term care insurance, thinking instead that they're preserving assets for their family, rather than spending them on insurance. Many people also don't understand that Medicaid, a means-tested program that is tied to one's income, is a back-up payment method that requires that the insured essentially be poor or that the person must "spend down," or become poor, to be eligible.

I have since learned that Medicaid, the government program that pays for health care for low-income individuals, covers only about 13 percent of assisted living residents nationally, compared to about two-thirds of nursing home residents. Moreover, there are large disparities among states as to the level of financing provided to those elders eligible for Medicaid.

The cost of an apartment in assisted living varies tremendously around the country. The average cost for a single occupant is $36,264 per year. According to researchers Rosalie Kane, Jane Chan, and Robert Kane (2007) the mean charge for an apartment in assisted living can ranges from $1,606 to $2,379 per month. But the Assisted Living Federation of America (2013) projects an average cost for a private one-bedroom apartment at about $3,000 per month.

According to health policy researcher, Robert Mollica (2009), twenty-four states supplement the beneficiary's federal Supplemental Security Income (SSI) payment to cover such costs as room and board. State supplements vary widely, from a state like Oregon, which has five payment levels ranging from about $1,000 per month to slightly more than $2,000 per month; to Ohio, where room and board are capped at $624 per month. And some states provide no additional payments. Twenty-five states allow family members—or third parties—to supplement the payments of room and board charges. Nonetheless, for those low-income, frail elders who cannot continue to live independently but do not want to live in a nursing home, the system is still inadequate.

We were fortunate because, despite my father's working-class roots, he had "married into money," something he never truly acknowledged but from which he certainly benefited. Although my mother's family business had been less lucrative than she expected or hoped, still she had steady unearned income that fueled a middle-class lifestyle for all of us. Having grown up poor and survived the depression, my father was a saver and, with the help of his accountant brother, had invested this money wisely. We were able to use money from the sale of our father's home as well as piece together his long-term care insurance and savings to pay for an apartment at Harmony Village. This level of security eludes many families in need of quality elder housing.

When our father was still living in his own home but no longer able to drive, my sister and I asked two of his dear friends, Paul and Leigh, if they could take him to medical appointments and to the grocery store on a weekly basis. Both of them were retired and available, even though they were still very involved in the theater community and other endeavors, and were glad to oblige. We worked out a mutually agreeable payment system, since it was more than just an occasional thing, and everyone felt comfortable with it. The rides were simply an extension of many years of relationship-building, and actually enriched the connections between this couple and our father. Moreover, they provided him with built-in regular companionship each week.

When our father moved to Harmony Village, this arrangement was easily transferrable. Leigh and Paul supplemented these "work trips" with unpaid outings to the theater and restaurants. We viewed these "outings" as social, and part of their personal relationship, as distinguished from necessary outings that were focused on providing care. It was a tenuous distinction, but seemed to work. And, although Harmony Village provided a weekly van for shopping and social events, my father chose to stick with his dear friends, who helped maintain the continuity of his previous life while he was in Harmony Village. I observed other residents busily chatting among themselves as they prepared to get in the van, but I knew my father refused this form of transportation because it felt too institutional. He didn't want to be herded into a van with other old people.

After a while, my father found it too exhausting to leave the facility for these shopping expeditions with friends. Along with continuing to take him to medical appointments, Leigh and Paul began shopping and doing other errands for him, such as picking up medications from the local drug store. His friends also spent more time hanging out with him at Harmony Village and escorting him to activities like exercise class and bingo in the facility. The purpose of their visits then focused more on simply providing companionship, and for the most part, he was grateful.

Despite the flurry of available activities at Harmony Village and a regular stream of visitors throughout the week, my father remained lonely and depressed, cognitively "with it" enough to know that he was fading, but not energetic enough to remain engaged to the degree that he desired. "What is the purpose of my life?" he would ask. My sister and I felt driven to remind him of all the people he had touched over the years, and the people still "in the room," literally and figuratively, people who loved and admired him. Sometimes our reassurance worked; other times, it did not. Gradually, we began bringing in private caretakers to cushion the loneliness during the days and times that Paul and Leigh couldn't be there.

Initially, we contacted Zora, a private caregiver who had cared for my uncle in his final year of life. Zora was a strong woman in every sense of the word—tall and majestic in stature and grounded in wisdom and experience. My father had seen her in action when she was caring for his younger brother, Maurie, and admired her intelligence and wit. "If I ever need that type of care," he told us, "see if you can bring in Zora." Our hope was that she would be available, but as luck would have it, she was busy caring for another elderly man. Instead, she brought two friends to meet with us, just a few members of an "underground network" of private caregivers, African-American women who were devoted to caring for elders and paid under the table for their work.

As it turned out, the first person we hired didn't work out. So once again, we called Zora, in hopes that she was available now. The irony was that her availability would mean that her former employer had passed away. This was the nature of her work. Her job was to build strong relationships with the elderly people she cared for, and then they died. We wanted her to be the person who helped us face this inevitable ending. This time when we called her, she was free.

Zora started spending long hours during the day with my father, and just as we expected, she was fantastic. Talkative, bright, and engaged, she was the perfect companion for my father, who sincerely enjoyed her company. I believe that they actually had fun together, even as he slowly slipped away. Zora had had a previous career working in hospital administration, and her current job as a caregiver, which she now did full time, was her so-called retirement career. On top of this work, she was also caring for a very ill husband, but she had the help of an adult daughter who had moved back home and who brought her tremendous joy.

Despite Zora's positive presence during the day, my father struggled with insomnia every night and ended up sleeping much of the day. Zora was the first to offer her interpretation: "I think he's afraid of dying." Maybe it was the dark or the quiet or the lack of social interaction or all three. Maybe it was his deep fear of being alone, or his fear of what might happen without someone watching over him, protecting him. Maybe he was obsessing about whether his life was still meaningful, or in a moment of confusion, was trying to figure out what he was doing at Harmony Village, this house of apparent strangers. Or maybe he was revisiting his past and questioning whether he made the right decision sixty years before when he challenged the House Un-American Activities Committee. Or maybe he was simply worrying about whether he could get to the bathroom on time without peeing in his pants or falling flat on his face, and then what? Maybe, maybe, maybe . . .

We will never know what was going through his mind. But what we do know was that every five or ten minutes, he started ringing the special alarm that hung on a loose rope around his neck—like an albatross that he begrudgingly needed. I imagine that if his favorite aide, Janelle, was on that night, he got some relief. She was sensitive, compassionate, and gentle, and she knew how to put him at ease. But if it was Janice or Sarina, I'm sure it was a different story. They would have been annoyed, and told him to "stop ringing that bell." This would have only increased his anxiety and made him feel even more alone. I know that the next day, all memory of an unpleasant night was erased because I would ask him, "How was the night, Dad?" and he would reply with feigned gusto, "Very good, very good!" One time he said to me, with a slight smile, "They tell me that I'm not sleeping at night, but I don't remember a thing!" Maybe that was okay. Why should we remember the painful times, especially as we fade away?

It was only after this pattern was sustained for a month or so that the head nurse gently told me, "Evenings are your father's hardest times. Maybe it's a good idea to bring in an evening caregiver." I sensed that Harmony Village could ask him to leave if we chose not to take her advice. He was straining the system. Assisted living at Harmony Village was not equipped to provide round-the-clock care. That type of care was what you'd get at a nursing home. But they were giving us an opportunity to supplement the care they provided to avoid yet another move.

So once again, we went back to Zora and asked her, "How about nights?" We were just lucky that she either enjoyed the work, needed the money, or both, because she replied, "That would be just fine. We'll have a good time." Without pause, Zora slept over that night in my father's apartment, settling in a chair, claiming that it was "no problem." The next day, my sister and I ran out to a local furniture store and purchased a cozy, beige, small fold-out couch that became Zora's bed for the next six months.

Zora also called upon her network of caregiver friends again, bringing in Rosie and Lila and another caregiver who ultimately didn't work out. These women alternated evenings so that my father always had a caregiver with him in the evenings. Once again, we appreciated the fact that my father had adequate resources that allowed us to supplement his care.

Despite my ambivalence toward religion, I felt that these caregivers—all bound by their Christian faith—were like angels doing G-d's work. I felt taken care of in their hands, and I'm sure my father felt the same. Every morning they wrote a journal entry, reporting on my father's night. "He was up all night and we played music," or "He was restless and wanted toast at 3:00 a.m. so I made it and he went back to sleep." Or "It was a good night, but then I had a hard time getting him to breakfast." I discovered through both personal experience and observation that it is challenging work to be with an elderly man who is dying, to be present and responsive and not too pushy, but just pushy enough.

When I visited on the weekends, I noticed that everyone in Harmony Village knew Zora. She was warm and gregarious with all the residents and with the staff. And when the inevitable happened and she was offered a job at Harmony Village, she turned it down because she valued her autonomy.

As my father became frailer, he was increasingly vulnerable to falls. One time, Zora literally caught him as he tripped over his oxygen cord. "I'm your protector," she told him, and that title stuck. She was his protector, and from that point on, he felt that he was literally and figuratively in her hands.

Shortly before his death, my father had taken a fall on a night that Zora wasn't working. I think she still imagined that, had she been there, he would still be alive.

Memory Garden

Over the years, inspired by what I was learning about the power of integrating the arts into teaching, I began to incorporate theater into all of my sociology courses. My strategy was to pick a play that was relevant for the material I was teaching and then get students in the class to perform an act of the play. I had learned over the years that participating in an arts experience deepens one's understanding of the characters and encourages students to be more engaged. After the students acted in the play, we talked about it, using various sociological theories as a framework for discussion.

In a feminist theory class I taught at Tufts University, student actors performed one act of the *Glass Menagerie*, and then we analyzed what motivated the characters of Laura and her gentleman caller. Are their actions driven by their biology, or are they shaped by how society constructed their roles? Using theater gave me an entrée into these essential questions.

When I taught a class at the Massachusetts Institute of Technology (MIT) on gender, race, and work policies, I introduced a British play called *Gut Girls* by Sarah Daniels, in which a group of women slaughterhouse workers encounter an upper-class woman who wants to rescue them from their so-called demeaning labor. The shyest of students came alive when they read the lines of their characters, who swear and make crass jokes, which gave the students permission to act a little crazy. I was able to harness this excitement to facilitate a serious dialogue.

When I was asked to teach a sociology class on aging at my alma mater, Brandeis University, I searched for a play that could raise issues of aging without trivializing or demeaning old age. I considered Arthur Miller's *I Can't Remember Anything*, but despite the ironic title, I felt that the theme—that old people lose their memories—was simplistic and didn't have enough substance to sustain a deep theoretical analysis. Then I remembered a play called *Memory Garden* by Rebecca Ritchie, a talented writer and lawyer who had studied playwriting with my father in the Western New York Playwrights Workshop. Many years earlier, he and his good friend, Roz, had performed this play, and it was very well received.

Memory Garden has a simple but poignant plot, centering on a woman—formerly a landscape architect—who is dying of breast cancer and suffers from dementia. Her husband knows she is dying and wants her to hand over the power of attorney to him, a meaningful act signifying she is no longer able to make her own decisions. Ritchie's own personal narrative makes this play even more powerful, in that all the women in her family had died of breast cancer, a disease to which she, too, eventually succumbed.

Two students, an Orthodox Jew and a Chinese international student, volunteered to play the lead roles of Mim and Ben. Despite the fact that they were a most unlikely couple, they nailed the characters. Mim imagines a garden renovation and speaks in metaphors about tending the future. But when Ben pushes for Mim to give him the power of attorney, she resists. One of the most moving scenes is when Mim is digging furiously in her imaginary garden, and Ben, taking a cloth, tenderly wipes her face.

The student playing Ben's character pleads with her to sign the papers, saying, "Look, hon. I know you don't like to be pushed or hurried or made to do something you haven't thought through, but we're a little rushed here." I scan the room to see if any of the other students find this overly melodramatic, but no, they are entirely engrossed. Students seem to have forgotten that the performers are just fellow students in their Aging in Society class.

Mim replies dreamily, "I liked your eyes. I remember that. Soft blue like Forget-Me-Nots." The air in the classroom hangs suspended, as students witness the power of human interaction through drama. At the end of the play, even though we're sitting in a classroom in the sociology department, they cheer wildly. The discussion that follows about aging and end-of-life issues—in the context of these characters' lives—is rich and deep.

I remember when I visited my Uncle Maurie at the local Jewish nursing home, the one my father would never have agreed to live in. Maurie had always been talkative with his brothers, but had little to say to me or the other children, so I was startled at how chatty he was during my visit. "Which car do you think I should buy," he asked me. "The green one or the blue one?" I hesitated, confused, wondering if he was really about to purchase a new car. After all, he was living in a nursing home, and moreover, he was blind, so how could he possibly drive? And then I realized that I needed to get inside his story in order to communicate with him. Unlike Ben, in *Memory Garden*, the stakes were low for me to simply enter my uncle's illusory world. "I think the blue one might be better," I replied. And he agreed that he would buy the blue one. Like Mim, his mind was bending reality, but it was a harmless reality that somehow made sense to him and maybe even served to connect him to the man he used to be.

My father's hallucinations were a lot scarier. One night my phone rang at 2:00 a.m. I awoke from a deep sleep and ran downstairs, just grabbing the phone in time. "Min," he whispered, "I'm in a situation here." What's up," I asked him. "They're trying to get me, Min." Trying to remain calm, I asked him who was trying to get him, and he replied, "The people here," sounding terrified. "This place is terrible. They warehouse old people here, Min. They've locked me in.

You have to come right away and get me out of here!" I took a deep breath and asked him if he was alone, knowing that there was—or should be—a paid caregiver with him. "She's in the other room," he told me. "But she's with *them*." And then he whispered loudly, "You've gotta get me out of here right away!"

My living room was dark, and I lowered myself onto the couch, aware of the cold air, as I grabbed a nearby blanket and wrapped it around my body. I knew I must enter his world, as Ben entered Mim's, and as I entered the world of my Uncle Maurie. That was the only way I could reach him, to help him feel safe. I could see that he felt trapped, and the reality was that he was trapped on a road toward the inevitable. His paranoia—while not based in any real-time truth—resonated with his past experience of being followed by the FBI for more than three decades. Somehow, perhaps, he was conflating his deepest fears with the reality of his current circumstance.

I knew I could reach him—to speak to him as the daughter he trusted and loved. So I asked him simply, "Do you trust me, Dad?"

"Yes," he replied.

And I said, "I'm going to tell you what I think is going on. Will you listen to me?"

"Yes," he said.

I began. "You spent a lot of your life being pursued by the FBI. That was real. Are you listening to me, Dad?"

"Yes."

"There were people who tried to destroy you for many years, Dad, and you fought them throughout your life."

"Yes," he agreed.

"You are living in an institution now, Dad," I told him. "While it may have been better for you to live with us, it didn't turn out that way. When you were more together and your health was good, you wanted to stay in Buffalo. Am I right?" I asked him.

"Yes, right, Min," he replied.

"And now, you are in an institution where you don't have the same control you had over your life. And that is a real drag."

He agreed.

"But Dad, are you still listening to me?"

"Yes, Min," he said.

"No one is trying to 'get you' there, Dad. It may feel like that, but you are stuck in a place where you don't want to be, and that makes it feel like prison. But it isn't a prison. Are you still listening to me?"

"Yes," he said.

"And do you trust that I will tell you the truth?"

"Yes," he said.

I took a deep breath. Even though my sister and I are doing our best to ensure the best care for him, he is stuck in this netherworld, this purgatory between the life he actively lived and created and the very end of that life.

I asked him if I could speak with the caregiver, and she got on the phone. I discovered that his hallucinations were scaring her and that instead of focusing on his needs, she went into the other room, leaving him alone. She rationalized this response, telling me that he needed to be alone. I was furious. But I left that problem until later.

At that time, I told her to stay with him and then asked her to put him back on the line. I explained to him that the caregiver was there with him and would protect him. I reminded him that we loved him very much and told him, with a touch of guilt, that we would be seeing him over the weekend, a time that seemed light years away. And I reminded him one more time that he had a reason to be paranoid for many years, and that maybe his medications were making the situation worse, and that I would check on them as well.

After talking to him for more than an hour, he had seemed to calm down. Reversing the past roles of child and parent, I asked him, "Do you feel safe now?" "Yes, Min," he said. "And do you think you can fall asleep?" "Yes," he replied. We hung up, and I tried, with little success, to get back to sleep. Later, I fired the caregiver, and she didn't understand why, demanding severance pay, even though she had been with him for only a few weeks.

Writing and Secular Immortality

Every day throughout my childhood, my father set up shop to write at our dining room table, a large, heavy, blond-wood rectangle that dominated the room. His materials included a typewriter, white-out to correct typos, a box full of pencils and erasers, and an enormous reel-to-reel tape recorder that sat in the middle of the table. He moved back and forth from typewriter to pencil editing, and when he had written something he liked, he would tape himself reading through his draft script, playing all the characters, only slightly altering his gravelly voice for each one. The process was time-consuming, and he plugged away at it consistently.

Many years later, when giving me advice about writing, he told me that the most important thing about writing is to write every day. "Just get it down on paper," he would tell me. "Writing is rewriting." Little did I know that these private tidbits would someday be fashioned into semester-long courses he taught on playwriting to college students, labor union members, and community activists. He followed his own advice and returned to this table daily, churning out page after page. Until he died, we had no idea how much he had produced over the years: an impressive pile of plays, short stories, essays, and novels, most of which had been completed, including some that had never been publicly released.

Trying to get my father's attention when he was writing was impossible. He built an invisible wall around that large, rectangular table, and anytime I approached him, he would draw his body inward and move closer to his typewriter, banging on the keys, literally ignoring me. Whether I was asking him for permission to do something or wanted to tell him about my latest "A" on a quiz—because I always wanted to impress him—it didn't matter. He created his own small island and nothing could penetrate it.

If I persisted, he got angry at me because I was interrupting his concentration, his body growing tenser as he shouted out the obvious, a whispered, "I'm busy now!" And I would quietly walk away. I understand his frustration now, because writing takes concentration, but he was literally sitting in a room that was in the middle of our house, wishing he were invisible, wishing I would go away. To this young child, this behavior was a tease, having her father so close, yet so far away. I felt pushed away and hurt, but didn't have the words to express my feelings, nor would he have listened if I did.

Having a playwright father sounded pretty cool to my friends, but to me, it was not so cool until I was grown up. When I was about thirteen, one of his most successful plays, *The Dodo Bird*, was performed Off-Broadway. The play centers on three characters in a bar.

One character is an alcoholic who has been automated out of his job and is hanging out in a tavern waiting to see his long-lost daughter; the other two characters play angel and devil with the protagonist. One tries to get him to take a drink, and the other urges him not to so that he will be sober when his daughter arrives.

Having a play performed Off-Broadway was a big deal; that I knew. I couldn't wait to go to New York, which I had built up to mythic proportions in my mind. I was excited that we would be staying at a famous old hotel called the Croydon, known for housing artists and actors and other creative people. I imagined a beautiful building with ornate lights outside and a grand ballroom, something like the Park Lane but even cooler because it was for artists. Instead, what I found was a decrepit old building, sadly in need of repair. I remember crying ungratefully, "This is it?" To me, New York City was dirty and noisy. All the buzz about it seemed hollow.

I was too young to understand the play, and the universe it portrayed was foreign to me. I didn't know the world of bars, much less bars in working-class neighborhoods. The only bar I had been in was a cocktail lounge at the Park Lane, far different from the working-class tavern in *The Dodo Bird*. Moreover, the storyline was hard for a young child to relate to. While I could understand the pathos of a father waiting for his daughter, I wasn't familiar with gritty working-class guys, as my father portrayed them, sparring with words that had an undercurrent of violence. Nor did I grasp at the time that the main character might have any connection to my own mother, whose alcoholism wasn't apparent to us until much too late.

Although I couldn't understand the play at the time, I was not too young to be sensitive to audience reaction. I wanted people to like it or, better still, to love it and think my father was a brilliant writer. During intermission, I was small enough to slither through the crowd, to my mind, unnoticed, trying to overhear people's conversations. Sitting in a bathroom stall in the theater's ornate lady's room, I listened to a woman tell her friend that she thought the play seemed realistic. In that moment, I felt a small sense of relief.

After the play, we all went back to the hotel—my sister and brother-in-law, my father and mother and me—and got settled in one room, waiting for reviews to come out in the *New York Times* and the *New York Daily News*. We had picked up corned beef and pastrami sandwiches from a local deli, and eating them sort of helped to pass the time. Finally, my brother-in-law ran out to Penn Station, where you could buy the midnight edition of all the local papers.

As I reflected on this night, I'm amazed that my father stayed back with us, tense, saying very little, and appearing quietly terrified to read what reviewers had to say. If I were him, I think you couldn't have stopped me from running to Penn Station to get those papers. The air in that hotel room was thick with tension. Somehow, I feared that if the reviews weren't good, my father would be devastated, humiliated, embarrassed. I felt that a successful review would be redemptive, somehow—I didn't know exactly how—linked amorphously to his experience with HUAC, a public affirmation, perhaps, that he was right and HUAC was wrong. My brother-in-law returned with the papers and we hungrily read them out loud.

The reviews were tepid, and instead of the relief we were hoping for, a heaviness settled in that room, my father becoming even more internal. I think I would have preferred him to scream or yell or protest. But he just sat there in silence, and that, to me, spoke volumes. My father was always hard to read, but I felt that I had a special ability to read him. That was our connection, the distant father and me, the intuitive daughter. Nothing we could say seemed to buoy his spirits. And the next day we went home.

Over the years that my father's plays were performed, I felt a confusing mixture of emotions. I wanted his plays to be successful because I could literally feel his deep depression and disappointment when they were not. Our closeness was like that. Not good for either of us. At the same time, I often couldn't relate to the action on stage, with working-class characters I didn't know and conflicts that were unfamiliar. Some of his plays were transparent, openly displaying the dynamics in his family, often with him as the hero standing up for his beliefs against a backdrop of parents and siblings who were critical or unsupportive. These plays made me squirm with discomfort. I sensed that it wasn't right to portray his family so vividly and with such lack of compassion. And I hated seeing these characters on stage who looked and sounded like my aunts and uncles.

Once, my sister and I almost started laughing during one of his plays. "Hey, there's Uncle Maurie! And there's Uncle David," I said to my sister, as we stifled giggles from our seats only feet away from the stage. And after the performance, my father discovered that his siblings were furious with him. But he denied that the play was about them, claiming that the characters were composites that he created to tell a story. I had mixed feelings about those plays, but my simmering fear that he felt like a failure persisted. And I needed to save him.

One year, we went back to New York to see another production of *The Dodo Bird*, and this time, it was performed in an actual bar. Unlike in the past, I really listened to the play and began to understand the characters and the story. Maybe it was because I was older, or maybe the realistic setting made it come alive. But I was relieved. I liked it.

Some years later, when I was laid off from a job, I more deeply understood Dodo's anguish and despair. It felt like a punch in the stomach. And I instinctively turned to my father, knowing he would understand. Like a lot of people, my sense of self was linked to my identity as a worker. With that gone, I felt empty, useless, and hopeless. My father was able to reframe it all, "normalizing" the phenomenon of unemployment and convincing me that I had a right to unemployment insurance since I had worked for it. He helped me to restore my self-esteem and to feel hopeful that there was life after what felt at the time like a tragedy.

I turned to him for other job advice over the years, knowing that he would have a workplace analysis and some useful tips to boot. I'll never forget one time when I called him, right after a new boss had come into my workplace, a research center where I was directing a national study on flexible work policies in five large corporations. I had designed the complex study, solicited companies to participate, and traveled extensively to conduct interviews with workers. My coworker, who was supposed to do all the survey research, was slacking on the job, big time. I speculated that something was up right away, because every time I walked into his office, he quickly changed his computer screen to some random Microsoft Word document. And then a few moments later, my speculations would be confirmed, when I heard the hum of a shared printer, kicking out his latest travel plans or a receipt from his purchase of a new pair of running shoes.

After the new boss arrived and did a quick sweep to understand the lay of the land, she accused me of financial impropriety, which was shocking and preposterous. Initially, any reasonable dialogue with her was useless, and it didn't seem to help that many of my colleagues confirmed to her that it was untrue. I suspected that my slacker colleague was "misrepresenting" the truth in order to look good, although to this day, I have no real confirmation of that. This was the first time I had experienced such blatant betrayal in the workplace.

Until the allegations were cleaned up, I could barely breathe. Such was the level of my anxiety. But with my father's behind-the-scenes counsel, I fought the inaccurate charges, and ultimately, the new boss apologized to me for wrongful accusations. In the aftermath, I was furious at my deceitful coworker who maintained a friendly façade. But there was nothing more to do. When I left that job, which I did within months, I left with dignity.

As I cared for my father, I was flooded with memories of these moments when my father's counsel saved me.

Ultimately, after experiencing a slew of incompetent or bad bosses, I decided to run my own consulting business, which I began in the 1980s. My research continued to focus on workplace issues, an interest that felt organic, natural. No surprise, given that I grew up listening to my father's stories about labor and management struggles. But the slant I brought to my research and writing came out of my own experience as a mother and a worker.

I decided to write my PhD dissertation on parental leave policy and workplace culture because I wondered how the majority of workers in the US dealt with taking time away from their jobs when a new baby arrived. I felt lucky because I had the luxury of making my own schedule; most workers don't have that level of autonomy and control over their jobs. I turned the dissertation into a book, which I wrote late at night, between midnight and 3:00 a.m., after reading bedtime stories to our daughter and then grabbing a quick nap, unlike my father who certainly did not choose to wrap his writing around his family responsibilities.

Up until his fifties, my father had just one year of college under his belt. He came from a working-class family that could afford to send only two of his siblings to college. As he told the story, he wasn't considered one of the brilliant ones, like his brother Sam, who became a dentist, or his brother Martin, who became a university professor and Mark Twain scholar. After making his living selling life insurance for about fifteen years, and writing "on the side" at our dining room table, my father went back to school at Buffalo State College. Years later, he credited literary critic Leslie Fiedler, who was his advisor, with guiding him through a path that ultimately led to his getting his PhD in English.

I'm sure he took some courses, but as I recall, he was able to piece together a lot of previous experience for credit, jumping over hurdles, and sashaying through what could have been a long and arduous university experience. I can't remember him actually saying this, but our sense was that the university knew he was a scholar and just wanted to help him graduate.

When he finished, the university hired him as an assistant professor, evidence of the great admiration and respect his colleagues had for him, and which meant that he would be paid to write and teach. Within a few years, he was even tenured. Now that I have a foot in the academic world, I know how treacherous this process can be, but somehow for him, it seemed easy. Of course, this may have been a child's eye view.

Teaching is one of those professions that promise secular immortality, the notion that we achieve immortality through tangible accomplishments that continue when we are gone. If one is to measure one's worth by the impact he or she has on the next generation, influencing the minds of students is evidence of that contribution. Because of the tenure system, the university is one of the few workplaces where some people work until they are well beyond the traditional retirement age. This profession, which my father entered in his sixties, nurtured him until he was well into his nineties, which enabled him to continue to teach freshman composition classes to eighteen-year-olds as well as playwriting classes to older students. Over the years, many of his former students have approached me to say what a profound impact he had on their confidence as writers. And indeed, many of his former playwriting students became a part of his social circle.

These continued links to his past sustain me.

Boilermakers and Martinis

When my father was in his early nineties, he wrote and performed an autobiographical one-man show called *Boilermakers and Martinis.* The venue for his performances was a theater called Road Less Traveled in downtown Buffalo, which went on to produce a three-year cycle of his plays. *Boilermakers and Martinis* was a mildly scripted, mildly adlibbed narrative of his bifurcated life, split between his working-class world—symbolized by a tavern drink called a boilermaker, essentially a beer and a whiskey chaser—and the upper-middle-class world of my mother, symbolized by her favorite drink, the martini. He agonized over these two forces in his life, so diametrically opposed, and throughout the piece, he had a dialogue with himself about these two paths, wondering out loud whether he had done the right thing. Was he a good enough husband? Did he make the right decision to stand up to the House Un-American Activities Committee, despite the havoc it wreaked on our family? Was his life a life worth living? By the end of the performance, after much agony and hand-wringing, he concluded that he did, in fact, do the right thing.

Gerontologist Robert Butler (1975) first wrote about the importance of "life review" for older people, the process of reviewing and making sense of one's choices throughout life, and hopefully coming to terms with one's life circumstances and choices. Perhaps we are drawn to reviewing our lives as we near the end because we want to believe we have made a contribution to the world—or to our world, however large or small that may be. And perhaps we are drawn to a life review because it is one way to ease the inevitability of death. In her book, *The Ageless Self,* Sharon Kaufman postulates that older people construct themes that help them create a narrative for their lives. This narrative, in turn, gives their life meaning and a sense of purpose.

In her study of people with advanced cancer, researcher Meg Wise (2009) found that her interviews "elicited cancer and life stories that exemplified assets [people] built over a lifetime," providing "eloquent interpretive reflection on the meaning of [their] life and death." As she was conducting this research, her own father, a life-long painter, was dying. She helped him review the meaning of his paintings as a metaphor for his life, reflecting with him on the colors he used, the shapes he formed, and the subjects he chose. This process was calming for him, and strengthened the bond between them.

As a performer, my father used the stage as his vehicle to explore life's meaning. He chose to make his struggles public because he believed that they represented larger universal issues about class conflict and the ethic of staying true to one's principles. My sister and I—and our families—went to see him perform *Boilermakers and Martinis*, and unlike other times when we felt like squirming because we didn't know or understand the characters or, conversely, we knew the characters only too well, this time we listened in awe.

He had just had hip surgery about six months prior to performing the piece, and his recuperation was slow and frustrating. Again, his mood plummeted, and the only thing that motivated him was physical therapy, which he did religiously. Slowly his body improved, and when his healing plateaued, he cursed his body and questioned whether he should have gone through with this surgery in the first place. When he performed at the Studio Theater, only six months later, it was nothing short of a miracle.

Once again, the theater was my father's salvation, providing him with a venue to express himself, as well as a community of support and admiration. Every night of his performance, he climbed laboriously up the side stairs onto the stage. Once there, he grasped a walker with one hand and the arm of a stage hand who guided him until he reached level ground. As audience members watched this process, they literally held their collective breath. Once on solid ground, he slowly opened his walker, and without a pinch of hurry—because he knew the audience's gaze was riveted on him—he strolled to the center of the stage, where he simply sat at a table with a pile of 3x5 cards, telling his life story for an hour and a half.

For four weeks, five times per week, he performed this piece, and audiences were consistently and overwhelmingly moved to witness their very own local hero reveal his inner conflicts, and in so doing, pass on his greatest belief, that one must stay true to ones values and fight to make a better world. He wanted and needed to tell his story, making sense of his life night after night for four weeks of performances, a remarkable feat for a man in his nineties.

As it turned out, this performance was my father's swan song, the final major piece he would ever perform. But even as he was profoundly declining, and despite the inevitable, his spirit and aliveness was still evident.

Shifting Sand

As my father's health worsened, he became quieter, perhaps more internal, and certainly more inarticulate. His memory was less predictable, and his mood more sullen. Or, at least, this was how he behaved with me and other family members. Yet, when anyone from "the outside" came into his world, the performer in him was aroused, and he became more like his "old self": the actor, the storyteller, the wise old man. It was as though someone had pushed a button in his brain, and he would instantly recall stories from his past with great detail and vigor. When they walked out of the room, he would collapse into sleep, slumping into his straight-backed chair at command central.

A few years before my father moved into Harmony Village, we had contacted the facility to see if they wanted a speaker. They were delighted, and he gave an hour-long lecture to fifteen or so residents about the importance of bringing working people and labor issues onto the stage. Our strategy was to "normalize" the facility, allowing him to meet residents and see that not everyone was out of it or consumed with bingo. Although a number of residents in the audience dozed as he spoke, a few listened intently and asked decent questions. He walked away feeling that he had done a good job, and we hoped that this would translate to positive feelings about the facility, when and if he eventually moved into Harmony Village. When he finally made the move, my sister and I were desperately trying to figure out how he could maintain this connection to his theater community. Initially, we suggested that he teach a class about theater, piggybacking on his successful lecture. We had to remind him about this positive experience because time had all but wiped that memory away. However, by the time he arrived at Harmony Village, he had pretty much given up on the residents. He didn't want to find or create community in this final home. Moreover, he may have doubted his capacity to teach or perform at that point.

If he wasn't going to create a theater opportunity there, we thought that perhaps he would enjoy getting out of the facility to attend a theater performance. So we tried that. But it was exhausting for him to make the journey to the theater late at night, to sit uncomfortably for two or more hours, listening to the dialogue, and seeing little because of his failing eyesight. After these trips, he complained bitterly that the play was poorly constructed, attributing his confusion with the plot and the characters to a lousy performance. As his body and mind were winding down, his arrogance became his defense against recognizing his slow demise.

A few years earlier, one of Buffalo's progressive theater companies, the Subversive Theatre, had named their theater "The Manny Fried Playhouse," in honor of "Buffalo's own incomparable labor activist and theater artist." After my father had been living in Harmony Village for about six months, one of his friends from the theater contacted me, requesting an interview with him, which they would use in a fundraising video. He would bring a filmmaker to capture this interview. They realized it would be one of my father's last interviews. On the morning of the scheduled interview, I arrived at my father's apartment, only to find him lying in bed in a deep sleep. The facility's aide, whom we paid to dress him every morning, had not arrived. It was 9:00 a.m., only fifteen minutes from "show time."

As I began to wake him, the filmmaker called to say that the director's car wouldn't start. He was about to cancel because he was counting on the director to conduct the interview. But I told him that I would do it. After all, I interview people for a living. But more than that, it was hard for me to watch my father drift away, and it was somehow reassuring that, under a certain type of pressure, his mind could still become alert. I realized that I had been looking forward to this interview. It was yet another opportunity for me to see my father "come alive."

The filmmaker arrived half an hour later and began to set up. Meanwhile, my father sat hunched over his table at command central, slowly eating a bagel with cream cheese, a few slices of apple, and drinking a cup of coffee. He was in his own universe, focusing all his attention on eating and completely ignoring our guest. Given that he could no longer see what was on his plate, I often would orient him. And with the filmmaker watching intently, toying with whether he should begin filming but wanting to be respectful, I told my father, "The bagel is at twelve o'clock, and at three-o'clock, there's a bunch of apple slices. Your coffee is on the far right, opposite two o'clock."

Following these instructions, my father began to map out his plate and devise a strategy to tackle the meal. Slowly, his gnarled hands, embodying years of life and struggle, reached out tentatively in hopes of encountering an edible object. One hand guided his fork tenuously toward a shape he could see on the plate, his eyesight pierced with a dead zone due to his macular degeneration. He stabbed persistently until fork and food were connected.

I reminded him that his friend from Subversive Theatre was there in the room, and that pretty soon I would be asking him some questions about his life for the organization's fundraising video. I appealed to the performer in him, hoping this would tantalize him. But his plate remained the sole focus, as he slowly ate his breakfast, reminding me of psychologist Abraham Maslow's hierarchy of needs. Food first; then he just might shift his focus to other demands. It also occurred to me that he had an audience that wasn't going anywhere, so why should he hurry?

After about ten minutes, with the filmmaker growing increasingly anxious about whether they would ever begin, I suggested to my father that we start the interview while he was eating. He looked up at me and said, simply, "Okay." The light had suddenly turned on again in the theater of his mind. My father was ready to tell stories about his past with great detail and vigor.

My father's voice was commanding. Anyone who knew him would know what I mean. It had a gruff quality, but his enunciation was impeccable. He spoke with authority, and when I was a child, I never doubted whether he was right. As I got older, I realized how ridiculous this was. Yes, he *thought* he was always right; he argued well; he spoke with deep conviction about politics and the arts. But he wasn't always right, despite his assured delivery. He was a tough arguer, a vocal muscle you would want to have on your side. He read a lot and synthesized what he read into coherent and powerful analyses of political, economic, and social issues. His many years of acting only strengthened this ability to cultivate an argument and to modulate his voice to ensure the most dramatic and effective presentation.

Up until a month before he died, he could still use that bellowing voice. Anyone who knew him still misses that about him. To this day, I can conjure up his voice as though he were in the room.

In the interview, I asked my father questions about his work as a labor organizer. Given my own background as a researcher, I was comfortable probing his choices to write plays and stories about the struggles of working-class people. I knew that this was something Subversive Theatre wanted him to discuss. I also knew my father well enough to offer prompts that would awaken some of his memories. Knowing that they were hoping for a plug to use at their fundraiser, I asked him what he felt about the work of the Subversive Theatre. Without hesitation, he spelled out why he felt the theater was making an important contribution, just exactly what they wanted to hear!

Following the completion of the interview, the filmmaker and I went into the hallway to debrief. "This might be his last interview," he said to me, with both concern and awe. He had just observed my father's precarious health, and the intensity of talking to this dying man, one he so deeply admired, struck him hard. Over the next few months, my father surprised us all, as he stepped up to the plate for several more interviews, another award dinner, and a reading at a local bookstore. He wasn't ready to die.

Three months into my father's stay at Harmony Village, the Buffalo News published an article about him, written by Colin Dabkoski, called "Manny Fried: The First 100 Years." Promptly, the article was posted on the bulletin board, alongside obituaries and other important news such as large-font lists of the day's activities. With such a prime location—the bulletin board was situated across from the beauty salon and next to the line-up of resident mailboxes—many people strolled by the area daily. Prior to this public display of the article, he was like any other resident there, unknown, someone who may have had an interesting past or maybe not. Once there was a public article about him, the buzz began.

It was subtle at first, a nod in his direction, which he couldn't see because of his poor eyesight. Then a remark here and there from staff: "Mr. Fried! That was a great article about you!" Or a resident telling him they liked "the excellent article." One woman, passing him in the hall, told him, "That was so interesting! I had no idea!"

And another commented to a friend, "He's such a gentleman." My father acted as if he was oblivious to these remarks, but he couldn't resist smiling.

For most of the time he lived at Harmony Village, my father chose to be invisible, perhaps a way to passively resist being identified with the institution. "I am not like these people," he would spit. But this publicly displayed article brought his past into the building and gnawed away at his resistance, as others recognized his past as a part of his present. The outside world—in which he was considered a powerful and influential figure in the city of Buffalo—began to align with the old man who was a temporary resident at Harmony Village, stuck in the same limbo as everyone else.

HUAC 3

When I was in middle school, my parents had become close friends with the Swados family. Sylvia was my mother's best friend, and her husband, Bob, was a hotshot lawyer who represented sports teams and the local equity theater. Their daughter, Liz, was one of my best friends, and I spent a lot of time in their house, an old Tudor on a fancy block across from Delaware Park. My mother and Sylvia confided in one another over far too many drinks at the Park Lane, both creative women married to men with domineering personalities, depending on one another for emotional support and solace. Liz was different from my other friends, a composer at an early age who made up sad, philosophical songs that entranced me, like my favorite, "If every human could be a tree, reaching towards eternity, with an age infinity . . . what a world this would be." I remember us howling that one at the top of our lungs.

Liz and I had many sleepovers where we giggled all night, sang and made up wild stories, and ate way too many Toll House cookies. She taught me how to play guitar, and with great generosity, lent me two of her guitars, including a Gibson 12-string, when she went on vacation. As a young teenager, Liz rebelled against her parents, falling in love with a working-class guy who was the antithesis of what they wanted for their child, but to their credit, they allowed him into her life and home. I am still indebted to Liz for teaching me about sex, juxtaposing these lessons with doing our shared job as line captains in eighth grade, where we kept young children, as the title denotes, in a straight line outside our elementary school, PS 64, before we all filed into school.

When my father was subpoenaed by HUAC, Bob pulled the plug on this friendship, refusing any contact with my family and ordering his wife, Sylvia, to cut my mother off completely. Understandably, my mother was devastated. Slowly, she lost more and more of her upper-class Jewish friends, a pariah through no choice of her own. But throughout both times my father was subpoenaed by HUAC, she chose to stick by him. Two years later, Sylvia committed suicide.

One day, when my father was sitting alone at a table in the dining room at Harmony Village, another resident rode silently up to the table in his electric scooter. The visitor loudly announced his name, adding, "I'm blind, so I can't see you. What's your name?"

My father told two versions of what happened next, and depending on who you were, you got one version or the other. This is what he said to me in a brusque, powerful voice, the voice of the public figure who survived the wrath of HUAC: "He said his name was Bob, and I froze! I took the Fifth Amendment! I decided I didn't have to respond on the grounds that it may incriminate me. We sat there in silence, not speaking. I REFUSED to speak to him, the bastard!"

And this is what he told some of his friends, speaking calmly, emanating wisdom and humility: "I just told him my name. What's the point in making a big deal after all these years?"

It had been nearly seventy years since he had testified at the HUAC hearings, and he still had a bifurcated view of his past. One part of him held on to the pain and suffering he experienced during those years; the other part of him was able to let go of them and move on. Those two parts resided side by side until the end.

It's funny how the hodgepodge of one's life can converge in the dining room of an assisted living facility, not only for my father but for me as well. It turns out that Bob's room was down the hall from my father's, and I started wondering if I would run into his daughter, Liz. We hadn't seen each other for more than thirty years. I discovered that it was easy to track her down. She was a teacher and well-known composer, so I sent her an e-mail invitation to reconnect. After a half-century hiatus, Liz and I met in the hallways of Harmony Village, and we spent an hour in awe of our circumstances and the women we had become. When I told her about our fathers' dining room encounter, Liz commented, "Unbelievable, right? When my father told me, I screamed with laughter. Not to be insensitive, but the gods do play funny tricks. Thank god they're too old to punch each other out."

Immigration

My father came from a long line of survivors. Consider his mother. She came to this country from Hungary around 1890 from the small town of Nagy-mihályi in the county of Zemplén Megye, an area swept by war and politics that later shifted the town's borders, making it part of the independent Slovak Republic. According to my father, his mother made her journey alone at age fourteen, living for a time in Manhattan with relatives who had already emigrated, until she reversed her trip, returning by boat to Hungary to fetch her own parents and other relatives.

"My sister and I were supposed to return to our small Hungarian city where we were born," she later recounts in a short journal entry my father encouraged her to write. "My grandmother came because their younger children were here. However it fell to be my duty to help get the family to this country: my father, mother, two brothers, and my younger sister."

My grandmother's obituary says that she immigrated to America in 1895, not alone, but with her parents, a young woman at age eighteen, approaching marrying age. The retelling of history is an interpretative enterprise, but I would bank on my grandmother's memories. Either way, young or slightly older, alone or accompanied, my grandmother joined the ranks of thousands of immigrants who passed through Ellis Island, hoping for a better life.

Later, from the end of World War I until 1939, my grandmother's hometown became part of Czechoslovakia and was renamed Michalovce. But, once again, with the fall of the Czechoslovak government, it reverted back to the Slovak Republic, where it is now the largest town in the Michalovce *Okres* (district) in the Košický region of Slovakia. My cousin, Robin, who earned a PhD in Slavic Studies and is a fluent Czech speaker, first uncovered this bit of history and can actually pronounce both of these town's names correctly.

My grandmother Pauline's journey to America was prompted by the same circumstances that inspire immigrants to America these days: poverty and prejudice. Swept up in a wave of Eastern European Jews who were looking for a better life on these shores, she never shared the details of her actual trip because she didn't like to talk about "the past." When she was hospitalized with a broken hip later in her life, she suddenly began to remember the words to songs from her elementary school, which was called "normal school." When I said to her, "Grandma, that's amazing! Can you sing a verse?" she snapped at me in her thick Eastern European accent, "I don't have to sing it! It's enough that I remember it!"

Years earlier, when my grandfather started telling me about his childhood in Hungary, she barked at him, "Sol! She doesn't want to hear what happened so long ago!" a comment I regret to this day. Maybe she didn't think their stories of long ago would be of interest to me. Or perhaps the past was too painful to revive. But now I wish I knew.

Like thousands of Jewish immigrants, my grandmother's family settled in New York City, and during her teen years, she became a skilled seamstress, working in sweatshops by day and studying clothing patterns by night so that she could master the skill. I am grateful that my father implored his mother to write down her life story, but I struggle to decipher her seven handwritten pages that total three or so typed pages. I want more. Instead, I piece together my father's stories about his loving mother with her short narrative, both capturing her strength and fortitude.

My grandfather came from Bardejov, a city near the northern border of Poland that banned Jewish settlement for hundreds of years. By the 1800s, a strong Orthodox Jewish community had been established, with a "communal compound" situated outside of the town walls that included a study house, a ritual bath, and a well-known Hebrew printing press, lauded far and wide. The Jewish population continued to grow to more than five thousand, until World War II, when thousands of Bardejov Jews were deported to and killed at Auschwitz. I'm sure that my grandfather and many other Jews counted their blessings to have escaped this fate, and they undoubtedly knew families that were not so fortunate. My grandfather became a Talmudic scholar, likely nurtured as a young boy in this richly religious environment. But after coming to New York, he became a businessman, a good prospect for a nice Jewish girl like my grandmother. They met, not in Hungary, but in New York City.

Like many Ashkenazi Jews, my grandparents settled in the garment industry, probably because that's where they could find jobs, albeit with poor working conditions and low wages. Together, they opened a "dry goods" store that sold fabric and clothes and other knickknacks. By then, she had become a master seamstress. My father loved telling this part of her story, which allowed him to *kvell* (feel happy and proud) about his mother's skills and acumen. But pretty soon after my grandparents were together, she began having babies, barely taking a break between the birth of one child and becoming pregnant with the next. By the time she finally stopped, there were nine children. As the mother of one child, I cannot fathom the sheer physical burden of birthing so many children, much less the imperative to feed and clothe them.

I try to imagine how my grandmother juggled the care of her children with her sewing work and the running of the dry goods store, but for her, I don't believe it was a struggle; it was simply the way things were. In her journal, she wrote,

> When my mother and my friends asked why I decided to work so hard, I told them, "so I can relax when I'm old." Some asked, "do you think your husband will appreciate you?" I said I was sure he would.
>
> In Buffalo, I worked in the store. We had kitchen [help] so I could take care of my family while working in the store. [My husband] used to help with sending the children to school. After, [he] worked as a salesman selling yarns mostly in Niagara Falls while I ran the store, preparing meals in the evening, and taking care of laundry. I had to iron thirty shirts a week. Yet I did not complain. I was young and ambitious, looking for the future, hoping for a better tomorrow.

My father claimed, with some resentment, that his parents were absent, leaving the oldest to care for the youngest. Children aren't really equipped to be primary caregivers for children, and my father implied that some of his siblings took advantage of their power. At the same time, he loved his siblings and joked that there were always enough kids for a baseball team.

Stories about my grandfather were spare, but my father loved telling the one about my grandfather faithfully handing over money to his cousin to invest in an insurance policy that would protect the dry goods business in case of a disaster. When tragedy struck—a fire burning the entire building down that resulted in the loss of the business—my grandfather was pleased that he had made this wise investment. But when he went to his cousin, he was shocked to discover that the money had never been invested; instead, it had gone straight into his cousin's own pockets.

Listening to stories about their lives, it seemed that one tragedy was layered upon another. My grandmother wrote matter-of-factly about the "polio year" when they shared a house with a family in which all the children had contracted polio. "We could not let the children play together," she said. "The panic was tragic." When her husband—my grandfather—"took in a partner" against her strong objections, they lost everything, again. The partner "was not only a bad manager but a thief who carried out merchandise."

At the conclusion of these stories, my father would say, "My father told me that 'when you fall down, you get up,' and that's exactly what they did." The moral of the story was that horrible things happen to people, but one must soldier on. There is no time to wallow in the mire. This credo—that we must persevere despite adversity—inspired him throughout his experience with the House Un-American Activities Committee, and continued to drive him throughout his life.

Of my father's nine siblings, all of them ultimately "made good," achieving the American dream of sorts, at least on the face of it. There was one dentist, one factory owner, an accountant, an architect, a schoolteacher, a bookkeeper, one civil servant, and two English professors, my uncle and my father who taught at the same university. My father retired from this job in his nineties, after having several other careers. Of the nine children, at least one was a millionaire. He had invested his income wisely. The first two children married non-Jewish women, which prompted my grandfather to burn a suit in effigy for each of them, symbolizing the death of his sons. Later, one of them divorced and married a Jew, and the other one married another non-Jew. At that point, my grandfather could no longer afford to burn another suit, and I'd like to think that he finally accepted that the world was changing.

All but one of the nine children had children of their own, totaling twenty-one in all, meaning that I have a lot of cousins. Collectively, we all have had more than twenty children, and on and on it goes as the next generation has begun having their own kids. Each successive generation is one more step away from their heritage, and yet most have tried—in their own ways—to maintain a connection to their history as Jews.

How many families in America have their own immigration story? Either they come to this country from foreign soil or their parents came or their grandparents came to create a better life for themselves. They may be fleeing political persecution or religious persecution or poverty, or all three. And when they come here, they struggle to learn the language, to gain new skills, to find jobs, and to live the American dream. They work very, very hard. Many experience discrimination, often from people who feel threatened by them in some way or who want someone else to be lower on the totem pole. As Jewish immigrants from Eastern Europe, my grandparents were Caucasian. Although they didn't experience discrimination because of the color of their skin, they surely experienced discrimination because they were Jews and were poor.

Both of my father's parents were Orthodox Jews who closely adhered to their religious beliefs and rituals. When my grandfather retired, he became the scholar in his Shul, the Orthodox synagogue to which he belonged. My grandmother's role was to cook and clean and care for him and any other family member in need.

When my father was about eighty-five, my sister and I organized the first of several family reunions. Approximately sixty relatives came from around the country, as well as from Israel and Guam, and for the first few days, we just stared with wonder at one another while we absorbed our genealogy, from poor Jewish immigrants to middle- and upper-middle-class Americans living in contemporary society. To date, we have had three family reunions, each one with diminished numbers of our elders.

At the last reunion, the four remaining elders "held court" on a small couch, responding to questions about their life growing up in the Fried family. True to form, the siblings—my father, his youngest brother, and his oldest sister—squabbled about details of their past. "Remember the German Bund down the street from our house," my Aunt Sadie asked innocently. "There was no German Bund down the street, Sadie," snapped my father, as he and my uncle chuckled about her growing dementia. The German Bund was a pro-Nazi group, and she was beginning to imagine things. Fifteen minutes later, my aunt repeated, "Remember the German Bund down the street from our house." And again, the two brothers laughed.

Even though there were times I felt alone in the process of saying goodbye to my father, I knew that my cousins—now dispersed far and wide across the country and in other countries—knew and loved my father, as I knew and loved their parents. It was daunting to think about that generation being gone, as we were to inherit the work of sustaining our family, a role my father and some of his siblings took very seriously.

Injuries, Pain, and Depression . . .

After a hearty meal of brisket or boiled chicken at my grandparents' house, all the men in the family would lay supine on the postage stamp of a living room floor, while only steps away, the women would scurry around in the small dining room and kitchen cleaning up, chatting incessantly. When I was little, this gendered configuration just seemed normal. As I got older and developed a greater awareness of gender dynamics, I was irritated with how lazy the men were. My grandfather was the lead slacker, slouching in his special, worn-out chair before *and* after the meal. Years later, I discovered that my father and all of his brothers had back problems. So did my grandmother, but lying down after cooking as well as cleaning up from the meal wasn't an option for her. My grandfather did not have that excuse.

Apparently, I inherited the back problem gene. Knowing that my grandmother and all the men in the family had this problem was somehow comforting. It wasn't my "fault" that I had a vulnerable back; it just came with the gene pool, and I was in good company.

When I was a child, my father's spinal problems were mostly invisible. That is the thing about back problems, often they are not evident. My father was not a complainer, and for the most part, he kept his body strong doing his "army exercises" and running our dog, Charlie, so only occasionally did his back pain kick up. But at one point, he traveled the ninety miles from Buffalo to Toronto to get a consultation from a spine specialist about his neck pain. It turned out that he had a pinched nerve, and there was talk about surgery. Instead, he came home with a medieval-looking traction device linked to a pulley system that he hung around his neck and attached to the top of a door, which provided nightly relief.

Like my father, I was an athlete, and the form I chose was modern dance. I started when I was seven years old, initially in a traditional ballet studio. But that lasted only one year because I hated the mean ballet mistress as well as ballet's rigidity. Realizing that her youngest daughter needed to move, my mother persevered until she found a modern dance studio that I absolutely loved. For the next ten years, I took four classes per week with Seenier Rothier, a wiry, ageless woman with a rock-hard body and a raspy voice who taught classical modern dance, Martha Graham–style. Her studio became a refuge to me, especially during the HUAC days when my entire cohort of friends rejected me because of my father's reputation as a "commie pinko." The dance studio was an oasis. When I was there, I felt competent and strong, and I had plenty of friends—like-minded, dance-obsessed girls just like me.

But dancers can't dance forever. Bodies age, and the movements that may seem simple one year require more warm-ups and practice the next. I continued to dance, but it was getting harder on my body. At first, I only suffered from typical minor injuries: a pulled muscle or a sprained ankle. But over the years, the injuries compounded, until finally, after dancing for nearly thirty years, I seriously injured my back. My injury was sustained on a ferry boat as I was returning from a two-week vacation in Nova Scotia. I had been ignoring signs that I was in trouble, particularly a sharp pain that radiated down my leg that I treated as a simple annoyance. In Nova Scotia, where a friend and I camped out on beaches and in parks, I continued to ignore the pain and kept on biking and swimming. It only worsened, but I soldiered on. I had learned this "skill" as a dancer, because it was part of dance culture, the belief or notion that one can "move through" pain, that it will go away without rest or intervention. My compulsion to continue exercising obscured reason.

At the moment my back snapped and I fell to the ground, I was pulling hard on the handle of a slot machine that was located on the interior deck of the ferry boat. Ironically, as my body collapsed, I was rewarded with a waterfall of quarters catapulting to the ground. The pain was so searing, so all-encompassing, that I paid no attention to where the coins ultimately landed. I assume some lucky person scooped them up. For the rest of the ferry ride, I lay supine on a wooden bench in the captain's quarters, covered in packs of ice. The ride back to the mainland seemed interminable, and once we arrived, we still had an eight-hour car ride to get back home to Boston. The prospect of that long drive terrified me because any movement was excruciatingly painful. But there was no alternative. For what seemed like forever, I laid on the back seat of the car, moaning with pain at every slight jostle of the car, worrying about what I had done to my body. I was desperate to see a doctor and get a diagnosis, and I knew instinctively that it was something really bad.

Ultimately, not a single practitioner was able to diagnose the problem conclusively. Maybe it was a torn ligament or muscle, maybe a herniated disk. Whatever it was, it took me nearly a year before I was able to walk again. Much of that year, I spent on the floor of my living room in a shared apartment, interrupted only by visits to various specialists, including doctors, chiropractors, masseuses, acupuncturists, and physical therapists. At times, I thought I was having a heart attack because my heart was constantly racing. Not until many years later did I learn that this was just a symptom of a panic attack, one that recurred in waves for many months.

At night, I dreamed that I was still a dancer, leaping high in the air across an infinite wooden floor. But when I awoke, I felt a dark veil descend as I came into consciousness and remembered that I was trapped in my body. I was no longer a leaping dancer, but instead a former dancer who could not move. My self-identity, wrapped up in the freedom of expression through movement, was punctured.

I remember one alternative practitioner telling me that this experience was an important opportunity to grow spiritually, and that just infuriated me. No one who is in pain likes to be told that it's a good thing.

Now—nearly twenty years later—I can say that the injury did change my life in ways that I could not have predicted, many of which were positive. At the very least, I have learned a great deal about the links between pain, anxiety, and depression. I would say it has served me well in understanding and having compassion for other people's struggles, including—and especially—my father's.

My father's moments of happiness were washed with a deep underlying sense of emptiness. Each of his many accomplishments seemed to stand alone, disappearing into the backdrop of a life that lacked connection. Despite his ability to paint portraits of complex communication among the people he wrote about, he lacked the capacity to unravel the complicated emotions he experienced in his own relationships. This left him feeling quite alone. When he suffered from loneliness and depression, I recognized what he was going through, and I believe he knew that, which I'd like to think was helpful to him. I was often able to listen and empathize without judgment, and I worked hard to find that sweet spot between listening, reflecting, and helping him problem-solve. I knew he would persevere, but I was sorry for his suffering.

When I, in turn, shared stories about my own struggles, he worried endlessly about me. He would offer prescriptive advice, relentlessly citing the same old edict, "When you fall down, you get up." Although his advice may have appeared pushy or demanding, I knew that it was driven by his caring. But the problem with that edict is that I didn't really understand it until I had accomplished it.

One day, when he was about ninety years old, my father called me, and speaking with his strong, reassuring voice, said, "Honey, I was in a small accident but everything is fine. I could have walked away, *no problem*, but they made me lie down and be carried by ambulance to the hospital. But don't worry. I am totally fine." He had been driving on a highway that cuts through the city and, from a distance, saw that a mattress was lying on the road. His initial impulse was that it was safer to drive over the mattress, instead of stopping short on the highway in the middle of busy traffic. What he failed to see was that the car the mattress had fallen from had stopped dead in its tracks, instead of pulling over to the shoulder.

Just as I had responded when I first hurt my back, my father tried to ignore the signs that he was injured. For a while, he really believed that he had walked away from the accident unscathed. The last thing he wanted to do in his life was slow down. My sister and I worried about him, but whenever we asked how he was doing, he blithely repeated, "I'm fine." We were not surprised when, over the next few months, he reported that he was feeling pain and numbness in his arm and was having difficulty holding objects. First he went to see Dr. Fine, who did some rudimentary tests but did not link the symptoms to the accident. To us, the connection was obvious, and we continued to monitor the situation.

Finally, after six months of increasing numbness and pain, he went back to Dr. Fine, who recognized that the situation was worsening and immediately sent him to have an MRI. As we suspected, it was serious: there was a bad tear in his cervical spine which required immediate surgery.

A local surgeon had promised that he could fix the tear in an hour-long surgery, but this seemed fishy to us. We suspected that the doctor was factoring age into his decision to do only an hour-long procedure, and we wanted a second opinion. Through some homework on my sister's part, our father was able to be seen by a top cervical spine surgeon based in Pittsburgh, my sister's hometown. Given our father's condition, we couldn't risk having him fly, so my sister drove to Buffalo to pick him up and then drove him back to Pittsburgh for a consultation with Dr. Kang. Rather than a one-hour procedure, the surgeon recommended a fairly complicated and immediate six-hour surgery to restore my father's cervical spine. Instead of seeing an old man on his last legs, this doctor saw a vibrant older man who, with the right intervention, could live many more years. The operation was a success, and my father spent the next two months living with my sister and her husband while he recuperated.

Not only were we worried about our father's health, but we also wanted to know if there were any other casualties in the accident. What about the driver of the car he hit? Were there any passengers? How did they fare in this terrifying accident? According to my father, there was nothing in the newspapers about it, and that apparently reassured him that no one was hurt.

During his recuperation, he again fell into a deep depression. His whole life had been defined by his productivity—as an actor, as a teacher, as a writer—but now all of that seemed impossible as he began the painstaking process of healing. Trapped in a rigid neck collar that allowed little movement and chafed chin and collar bone, he was miserably uncomfortable.

At least for the first month, he was stuck mostly in an upstairs room of my sister's house, as he wasn't able to move around easily, much less walk up and down stairs. As he worried about his demise, his mind tortured him. Anyone who has experienced the lethal combination of pain and depression and anxiety knows that it is hard to concentrate on anything productive in this altered state. He obsessed about his health, plunging further into the dark places of his mind. We eventually hired a caregiver to keep him company during the day while my sister and husband were at work. She administered his medications and drove him to physical and occupational therapy appointments. But he quickly grew to despise this woman, who could do nothing right from his perspective. He was angry and depressed, and she came to symbolize all that was wrong.

Gradually, he began to improve. He was able to remove the dreaded neck brace, first for short periods during the day, then gradually for longer and longer periods. Finally, it came off altogether. Instead of being holed up in an upstairs room of my sister's house, he moved downstairs to the dining room, where he spent much of the day. He began to read and watch a little TV. But mainly, he was a compliant patient, doing the exercises assigned by his therapists.

Every hour on the hour, he arranged a set of twenty quarters on the table, and one by one, he picked them up with gnarled fingers and stacked them in neat little piles. Once they were stacked, he rounded them up and started all over again, until he repeated the exercise three times. This exercise was alternated with squeezing a piece of an orange silly putty ball for ten minutes and doing a set of mild shoulder exercises.

The quarters were his mainstay, providing a small sense of accomplishment with every set of the exercise. As he began to see evidence of healing, the dark veil of depression began to lift, with a little help from the antianxiety drug Ativan, which he called "atta-boy." His sense of humor was returning, and everyone was relieved.

My sister and I refrained from asking if there was any information about the people in the car he had hit. Not until one year later did we discover that the driver sued my father for a million dollars, claiming that she had sustained a serious back injury and could no longer work. She had his age on her side. Surely, a ninety-year-old man would be at fault for the accident. But he counter-sued, citing her dangerous decision to make a dead stop right on the highway. The case languished in the courts for another year, until they finally settled. It was a wash, and neither of them owed the other. My sister and I were amazed at our father's capacity to block out the effects of his actions. Even if the other driver was to blame, we wanted him to care about her.

His capacity to believe he was right at all times contrasted with his self-questioning and persistent struggles with depression. And he carried this tension with him until the end.

Forage Bookstore

The drive to the Forage Bookstore on Main Street was uneventful. It could have been a ride to anywhere, with my father securely fastened into the seat next to me, peaceful and calm, dozing like a baby soothed by the gentle motion of the car.[2] I relished the smooth ride of the rental car, unlike my old jalopy at home that should have been retired years ago. But I was anxious. Before we left Harmony Village, I called Howard who ran the bookstore. "Please have everything ready for him," I said, knowing that my father would need to sit down the moment we arrived. His health was fragile, and I questioned whether he would be able to pull this off. I also talked to my father's publisher, Fred Whitehead, from John Brown Press, asking him to give an introduction to the audience about why he chose to publish my father's book *The Most Dangerous Man: A Personal Memoir*. No problem, he told me. Earlier, Fred had written to me, saying, "I realized that I really *have* to attend the book-signing at Forage on September eleventh. I've booked a flight to Buffalo arriving at mid-day on the ninth, and returning late afternoon on the fifteenth. During the extra days, I'd like to shoot some film around sections of Buffalo relating to your life. The aim would be a short documentary film, including the signing event."

I was, as always, puzzled by the intense devotion of my father's admirers. He was my father, a fallible human being, and for that, I didn't aggrandize him. But I could see it from both sides, and I was grateful that he was getting respect and attention at this stage in his life. Driving up Main Street, I was not sure when I should wake him. Did he need some time to transition? Should I wake him just as we arrived so that he would be more rested? I opted for the latter. He was not going to become much more alert anyway.

Getting out of the car was cumbersome. No matter how many times we did this, it was a struggle. From his seat on the passenger side, he shifted his body sideways in an awkward arc, his legs segueing to outside of the car and landing unceremoniously on the ground. The tubes of his oxygen tank must not get tangled as I angled my body in to help him shift his weight forward so he could stand up on his own two feet. He grabbed the side of the car with one hand and my arm with the other. With a grunt, he laboriously pulled his body upward, while I did the same from my stance on the street. Magically, he was vertical and appeared to be no worse for wear. I had already retrieved his walker, and it was open and ready to join him. I lifted the oxygen canister and put it into the front sack of his walker, as my father grabbed its metal hand bars. We were off.

The prospect of getting in and out of the car was always ominous, but sometimes it was easier than I imagined. That day, with luck, I had found a parking space only ten-steps from the store. If I walked this distance on my own, I would never have noticed the slight incline on the sidewalk. But with my father in tow, it felt like Mount Everest. "Are you okay, Dad?" I asked him. "Fine," he said quietly and glumly, glaring down at the sidewalk, as he put all his energy into each and every step. We finally reached the front door of the bookstore, which took some muscle to open. We walked in expectantly, but there was no sign advertising the book reading, no chairs, no setup of any kind.

The event would happen in half an hour. I was torn between standing with my father—who remained precariously on his feet—while hoping for an appearance by the bookstore owner, or running up to the counter on the other side of the room and leaving my father standing alone with his walker. Either choice was untenable. I went with a hybrid strategy. I held my father and shouted across the room for help.

Momentarily, Howard appeared. I was annoyed, and I told him

firmly, "We need a chair for him right this minute." My father quickly settled into a comfortable chair, closed his eyes, and dozed off again. Any stress in the situation had flown past him and knocked me right in the eye. As I looked at this sleeping soul, I could not imagine how he would be able to sign books shortly. Fred, the publisher, thankfully arrived on time, and I asked him if he was all set. He took a darting glance over at my slumbering father and his eyes momentarily froze as he assessed the situation. It was clear to him that his job was larger than he had imagined. I reassured him: "You do the introduction, and I will take on the rest. I'll welcome people, and even respond to people's questions on behalf of my father, if need be." By that time, Howard had set up a small card table, and I assembled the books neatly as he brought chairs from the back of the store and arranged them in a semicircle around the table. We were ready for whatever would happen.

Ten minutes passed, and we wondered if anyone would show up; then, slowly, friends and acquaintances began to file in, until about twenty-five people were present. A respectable number, I thought. I saw some of his old friends, people I had known for years, and I was relieved. In walked Karen, his warm and lovely artsy friend who ran a bed and breakfast, where in a few months, we would gather for a quiet family event following my father's funeral. Then there was the lesbian couple who, a decade before, had invited my father to be a speaker at their wedding; they would never forget his tribute to them. And there was Mike LoCurto, the city councilor, who several months later would give my father an award from the City of Buffalo posthumously, which my sister and I would gratefully accept. As the crowd gathered in a semicircle around the table where my father and I sat, a few stragglers came in, including a former creative writing student with a friend in tow.

Once people were seated, we began. Fred's camera was positioned to capture my father and his books, and I hovered by his side. For a moment, it felt like church. There was an air of expectation and a touch of solemnity. This was a friendly crowd, here to honor my father while he was still with us.

Fred's short introduction only reinforced this sentiment as he shared why he had chosen to publish my father's book. Earlier, he had e-mailed me, saying, "I'm so glad we 'made it' on this project.

It's a milestone for John Brown Press, our first full-length title." This was a big deal for my father, too. It was the first book he hadn't self-published, but I'm not sure he was able to appreciate it at the moment. Fred said, "I think [the book] is an important contribution in many areas: working-class autobiography, theater history, and labor history, to name a few." This was exactly what my father would want him to say, and I was hoping he was enjoying these words, even though he appeared to register nothing.

When Fred finished his remarks, he turned to my father and asked him if he'd like to add anything. I wondered if this was a courtesy or if Fred actually believed he would respond. All eyes shifted to my father. He shook his head, and simply said, "No." He was reserving his energy. A few people in the audience took the cue, realizing that there was very little juice left in my father. Something in the room shifted, and their alertness to his demise was tangible. Karen jumped up and ran over to hug my father, sitting next to him on his other side so that he was sandwiched between us. Unthinkingly, I moved closer to him as well. I asked the crowd if they wouldn't mind introducing themselves and including a word or two about how they knew my father. It was his turn to hear from them.

One by one, they spoke, grateful for an opportunity to honor him with their words. One woman in the lesbian couple said that my father was an inspiration and support to her when she was in a job crisis, and her partner shared the words my father spoke at their wedding. His former student thanked him for inspiring her to write, and her friend said she had been hearing about him for years. She was thrilled to finally meet the legend for whom she had so much respect. The city councilor rattled off some of the important contributions my father had made to the arts and to labor in Buffalo. And as each person said what they had to say, my father smiled and acknowledged their words silently. He didn't have to speak, only to listen. The grace of each speaker seemed to give him more life. Later, I found this note from Fred: "I woke up this morning thinking that Manny has become like a fierce Old Testament prophet. Interviewing him is like interviewing Isaiah."

One can lose one's sense of identity living in assisted living, a homey institution, but an institution nonetheless. The experience of the book-signing party at Forage should have reinforced my father's identity as a writer and teacher. But we would have to remind him of that again and again.

Fred e-mailed me a few days later. "The last morning I was there, I told Manny some jokes from my days as a welder. He laughed heartily. I think he needs that, some bits of humor, to lighten his latter days. I am so happy to have helped to see the memoirs into print, and to have had the experience of 'BEING THERE' for a few days. I mailed him a CD of some radio talks I did here, and will give him a phone call to see if he'd like some music, etc. That might help. I think if one sense 'goes'—sight in his case—one turns to the other senses."

I was touched by the kindness of his friends who wanted to help him live his last days or weeks or months with dignity, feeling seen and loved.

The car ride from the bookstore back to Harmony Village was peaceful for me. The book-signing party was a successful event in that nothing went terribly wrong and his friends got to give him some love. As for my father, he seemed glad it was over. He fell asleep the moment he entered the car, moved from car to bed as if in a daze, and slept for hours after getting home.

Always the Martyr

Being a union organizer during the 1940s and 1950s released my father from the dirty on-the-floor work, but he was better for having experienced that work. He knew firsthand what it was like to be on that side of the labor-management equation. That experience later became the grist for his plays, and the sustenance that gave him a sense of purpose. He had organized "guys" at Remington Rand, fought for and won better working conditions, increased wages for them, and gone out on strike with them. He also sold life insurance to them through a Canadian life insurance company after he was blacklisted and unable to find work in an American company. Through this job, he continued to hear about their challenges at work and their struggles at home. He had downed boilermakers—shots of whiskey chased by a beer—at the local tavern with these guys. He knew the people he wrote about and was passionate about telling their stories on stage. "No other contemporary playwright tells the story about labor like I do," he asserted. "There was Clifford Odets with *Waiting for Lefty*, and Arthur Miller with *Death of a Salesman*, but that's all."

This conviction—that he was the one contemporary writer who told the story of real working people on stage—fueled my father throughout his life. Never mind that he encountered so many obstacles. Over the years, he submitted his plays to numerous competitions and approached various theaters about getting a production. Whenever his work was rejected, he attributed it to his radical politics. If a play he submitted to a contest didn't win, he'd proclaim with great gusto in his strong, assured voice, "They're not ready for a play that tells the real story about working people!" emphasizing the word "real."

The fact that his work did not get the kind of prominence he desired didn't baffle him. He was convinced that he was simply ahead of his time and that one day, and most likely posthumously, his work would be discovered and revered. A confused mixture of self-importance and insecurity haunted him until he died.

Near the end, he asked my sister and me if we could carry on his work. "Min, you can do the editing and get the work into shape. And Lor, you can do the PR work." We had been given our "assignments" for when he was gone. My sister and I looked at each other and silently agreed not to argue. While we believed in him, and his life choices inspired us, he was also our father, a fallible man who often, unconsciously, put himself first. He loved us and cared for us, but his own narcissism sometimes got in the way. I could be flattered and annoyed with him at the same time. He respected my writing enough to give me this charge, but once again, it was a charge, and once again, he didn't acknowledge the importance of our own lives, our own families, our own work. Once again, we were told that even after he was gone, his work should come first.

Despite my annoyance, it was never simple when it came to my feelings about my father. He was usually there for me, particularly when I explicitly asked for help. As for the choices he made during the HUAC days, my sister and I unquestioningly respected our father's decision to stand up to the committee, and we respected his unflinching commitment to fight for the rights of working people. On many an occasion, I was proud to have a father who would stand up in a room full of people who were lost in the minutiae of an argument, who could quietly and clearly articulate the truth. He was our hero, and he was also a narcissist, a complex man whom we loved and respected who sometimes saw his world in such narrow terms—just us and them—without enough shades of gray.

Many years ago, when he insisted that his plays weren't getting produced because the FBI had warned off prospective producers, our initial reaction was to doubt: we wondered whether he was distorting facts to serve his own emotional needs. But then we discovered that the FBI *did* "visit" theater producers and they *did* stop some of his plays from being produced. And our irritation at his self-centeredness and grandiosity was tempered by the recognition that his paranoia was based in reality.

5

Coping with the End

Kindness of Strangers

After one of my weekend visits toward the end, I left my father's apartment at Harmony Village feeling both a sense of relief and a deep sadness, even though I knew I would see him in two weeks, assuming he was still alive. That thought evoked a grinding fear that choked my throat. I tried to convince myself that he would be all right and was being well cared for, even though he had renal failure, pulmonary failure, and congestive heart failure. This state of aliveness could not go on much longer. Driving to the airport was fairly straightforward in this small city, punctuated by my favorite junk food haunts, including the chocolate shop that fueled me through those emotionally taxing visits. I drove straight down Delaware Avenue, which passes from the adjacent suburb into the city of Buffalo, with little fanfare crossing the line, except for a gradual shift from streets lined with small businesses to the mini-mall with a Chinese restaurant called Tastes Good, and then a larger mall down the road with a Target and Office Max.

I always felt a bit nostalgic as I crossed Amherst Street, a minor thoroughfare where my father had lived alone in a small white house for more than twenty years, until a year earlier when we moved him into assisted living. Nearly half a century earlier, our family had lived in a fancier neighborhood across the Delaware Avenue line, but my mother would bring me to this very neighborhood to buy me clothes at a children's boutique shop called the Kiddie Koop. I shuddered as

I thought about the children's fashion show I was in, thanks to my mother, whose obsession with appearance didn't prepare her for the scourges of aging. Later, when I was a little older, I was allowed to walk the mile-long journey to the penny candy store next door to the Kiddie Koop. Those independent shops were long gone; instead, a gas station was on each of the four corners of the street, one of which housed a small generic grocery store where my father used to walk each day to buy a newspaper.

As I approached Amherst Street, the streetlight turned red, and I called my husband to let him know my plane was delayed. I flagrantly ignored the state's laws against using cell phones while driving, but moved quickly. If I got caught, I could feign ignorance. Suddenly, I felt a violent thump. My rental car had just been hit from behind. I muttered a profanity, and then remembered that my husband was on the phone and I told him that I had to go. My rental car was hit a second time! I instinctively moved my car into the next lane, just in time to avoid a third hit, as the offending car charged forward, hitting the car that had been in front of me. For a fleeting moment, I felt a sense of pride that I had moved out of harm's way.

My immediate concern was my own body, given my history of chronic back problems. But my body outwitted my anxiety, and I jumped out of the car. I was fine, but my rental car was not. The driver responsible for this reckless driving was an older man, probably in his eighties, who now sat frozen in the driver's seat. I approached him and, from a respectful distance, kindly told him to pull over. I jumped back into my car and followed him to the side of the road. He looked confused, unsure of what had just occurred and why. I discovered that he had borrowed his son's car to visit the gravesite of his wife who had died six years earlier. My guess was that he had put his foot on the accelerator instead of the brake. But he was in no state to verify anything.

Although the front bumper on his car was mottled, he didn't appear to be physically injured, although injuries from accidents have a way of creeping up on you. Of course, what would happen between him and his son was *their* next chapter, not mine. I could only imagine. Would the son continue to lend him his car? Would the man continue to drive? I sincerely hoped not, but I left that thought behind. I harkened back to my father's horrific accident a few years earlier, and I hoped that this more minor collision raised an important red flag for the man and his family. We were now connected by our humanness—he, grieving for the loss of his wife; I, grieving for the gradual loss of my father.

All I knew was that I needed to get out of this city, if only to have the physical distance from the reality of my dying father's life.

I experienced a similarly touching human connection when I arrived at the airport. The accident and its aftermath nearly made me miss my flight, and I hustled through security and raced to the gate, only to be told that the flight was delayed by twenty minutes. When I heard this news from the airline worker, I nonsensically blurted out my story and started to cry. For a moment, she looked me straight in the eye, and then she wrapped her arms around me and said, "I'm such a softy. I feel like crying with you!"

A week later, the airline gave me a $50 credit for the "inconvenience you recently experienced with us." I was grateful for this humane airline worker, and even for the airline that had garnered my loyalty with a simple gesture. But most of all, I was thankful that, in the midst of the challenges of caregiving, I encountered people—strangers—with whom I connected, who gracefully helped to diffuse those challenges.

Coping for Caregivers

One of my favorite films about elder caregiving is *The Savages*, a sort of comedy-drama in which two siblings—played by Philip Seymour Hoffman and Laura Linney—end up caring for their estranged, cantankerous, and largely negligent father as he is dying. Despite their anger at him, they chose to take charge of caring for him. In so doing, they are forced to negotiate their relationships with him and with each other. This powerful experience becomes an unexpected opportunity to face unresolved emotions that have blunted their personal and even professional development. The siblings turn to each other, amidst some sniping and deception. Ultimately, they find personal growth and a source of support in one another.

Caring for frail, elderly parents is stressful in the best of circumstances. In the case of *The Savages*, the siblings faced a worst-case scenario. Their father had clearly been horrid to them in the past, and they had chosen not to see him or each other for many years. Based on the nature of their relationships, one might guess that they wouldn't feel obligated to care for their father. Yet they came together, and they came through for him in the end. Why? One reason is that the notion of *filial obligation*—the sense of duty or obligation we feel to respect and care for our parents in their later and final stages of life—still prevails in our culture. Although this notion is more codified in some Eastern countries, it subtly inhabits our collective psyche.

Unlike the Savages, I was far from estranged from my father or our extended family. But the experience of caregiving was still hard. Knowing that a parent has relatively little time left is tough, and making decisions to maximize a parent's comfort and sense of well-being is challenging. In such circumstances, it is easy to put our own needs last, but I believe that that's exactly the opposite of what we need to do. I remember when I first traveled on a plane with my daughter and heard the flight attendant's instructions: "If you have a small child traveling with you, secure your mask *before* assisting with theirs." It made sense. We needed to take care of ourselves in order to ably care for others.

How can we do that? I discovered a number of ways to cushion my stress in the last year of my father's life. I'm sure there are many others.

I have a tendency to feel that I am alone, even when there are people around me. Sometimes I blame this tendency on the McCarthy era when I lost friends because of the ripple effect of my father's political stance. Other times, I think it's just a part of being human. In any case, I found that caring for my father forced me to recognize that I was not alone. Often we do our caregiving work in isolation, or we are forced to face difficult family dynamics as we negotiate the care of elder parents with our siblings. More and more of my friends and family members face these same challenges. But we are part of a "universal club" of adult children who struggle with caring for their parents, and we are far from alone.

In addition to being part of this broader community of caregivers, I experienced a new phenomenon: the concentric circles of support, which started with a small core and fanned out to a larger network. The inner circle included my immediate family, especially my sister, with whom I had to collaborate on a daily basis to sustain our father's emotional and physical health. The circle then broadened to include our spouses and children, who were concerned about our health and well-being, and beyond that to our generous cousins, who housed us throughout the entire year and with whom we became even closer.

Rather than resisting my visits, I began to look forward to being with these cousins on the weekends, as we rekindled our childhood relationships, bringing each other up to date with our adult selves. Whenever possible, my husband joined me, picking up some of the slack with my father, as my husband is also a playwright and was able to engage my father in theater talk.

Finally, the concentric circles spread out to our father's enormous social network, which included his theater friends, his activist friends, and his work friends and colleagues. My caregiver fatigue was buffered by these many layers of loving people, and I was glad of this.

In the beginning, I had some trepidation about how my sister and I would share the care. She is older than me, and there were many times in the past when she had been a surrogate parent to me, given that both my parents were distracted. Even though the dynamic with my sister had shifted over the years, I wondered what it would be like to "co-parent" our father together. Would she capitalize on her elder status, assert her own ideas and not listen to mine? Would she resist a collaborative approach? I had no reason to believe that this would be the case, but prior to taking care of our father together, we never had the occasion to act as a team.

Luckily, I found that, from the very start of our caregiving journey, it was an authentic partnership. Moreover, although I truly believe that my sister wanted to share the care, the actual volume of what needed to be done was so enormous that it was hard for either of us to imagine doing it solo. She discovered in me a partner who was game and had the chops to share the work equally, taking initiative when needed.

Despite our historic family dynamic, I had become a grown-up in my own world, capable of making decisions and thinking things through logically, holding down numerous responsible positions over the years, and parenting my own child effectively. This grown-up self—an independent woman who had a life quite apart from my family of birth—turned out to be a competent caregiver and advocate for our father. I realized that my sister and I had to be grown-ups to figure out the puzzle of caring for our dad, day by day.

Initially, when our father moved into Harmony Village, my husband and I were helping our daughter get settled in her dorm at college. My sister and her husband moved our father into his new home. They moved large pieces of furniture and sorted through the volumes of books, stories, and articles he had written and squirreled away in his closet. But once our daughter was established, I was able and ready to jump into the fray. I wanted to share the care equally with my sister. And we began to see that we could pinch-hit for one another if need be; surely there was enough work to go around.

Throughout the year, my sister and I talked on the phone regularly, sometimes several times a day. From the start, it helped to define and divide the tasks. As the older sister and executor of our father's estate, she had to deal with a mountain of financial concerns. Although she could resolve some issues on her own, she consulted with me about important choices we had to make along the way. These included costing out assisted living facilities, deciding on the best home for our father, and dealing with the long-term care insurance people who dragged their heels on reimbursing us for medical and housing costs.

Because these financial responsibilities were so time-consuming, I took on a number of other major tasks. For example, I coordinated all of my father's medical appointments and made sure he had rides to them. I scheduled private caregivers we eventually hired, and I resolved any issues that arose with them. I stayed in regular contact with the nursing staff at Harmony Village and coordinated my father's social calendar. I made sure that his friends were up to date on his well-being, and that he had enough company throughout the week.

Despite its burdens, caring for our father became a mission, and I believe that there were many times that we did better by him because we were doing it together. We simply didn't want to let each other down. And at times, it was fun! The behavioral traits that used to drive us crazy about our father became fodder for a good laugh. His grumpiness and narcissism were simply absorbed into an eye roll and a chuckle. We were getting perspective, and it felt pretty good.

Caring for an elderly parent often disrupts or puts a strain on other obligations. Adult caregivers are often challenged to put all or parts of their lives on hold. Throughout the time our father was living at Harmony Village, my sister and I maintained full-time paid work. The fact that we both work independently allowed us the flexibility to fold our caregiving work into our weekly schedules. Unfortunately, this is not the case for many adult caregivers who work for unsympathetic employers. Most workplaces still frame employees' elder care needs as personal problems, rather than as the universal social issue it has become, and too many workers are worried about jeopardizing their employment by talking to supervisors or managers about their needs for flexibility on the job.

According to researchers at the Families and Work Institute (Matos and Galinsky 2014), most workers opt not to discuss their caregiving problems with coworkers or supervisors, even though they may get to work late or need unexpected time off in order to iron out a caregiving challenge. And, at the policy level, the only safety net available to caregivers is the Family and Medical Leave Act, which allows employees in companies with fifty or more employees to take unpaid leave to care for an ill family member.

Working in an unsympathetic work environment only adds to the stress of an already stressful job. According to a 1995 study by Metropolitan Life Insurance Company (1997), elder care costs a company about $3,142 a year per employee, based on various costs associated with employee productivity. Yet companies wouldn't have to do a whole lot to hold onto their workers. Researchers at the Sloan Center on Aging and Work (Pitt-Catsouphes, Matz-Costa, and Bessen 2009) at Boston College argue that the main policy that positively affects worker productivity and commitment is scheduling flexibility.

I am quite certain that my flexible work schedule allowed me to remain productive in my paid work and in providing consistent care to my dad. Having control and autonomy over how and when I did my paid work facilitated my ability to devote unpaid time to my caregiving work, and probably lowered the level of stress.

Sharing the care and reaching out to a support network were powerful strategies to reduce the stress of caregiving. I also explored others. Taking long walks and using the local town gym helped abate my sense of feeling trapped at Harmony Village. At times, spending long weekends in my father's room did feel a bit like prison, and I was compelled to find ways to make the time pass. At first, I read books and magazines to him, but gradually, as his exhaustion deepened, he had a harder time understanding them, so I chose shorter pieces, and I read to him in shorter spurts. I found that it relieved my own stress to entertain him! We also watched some television, but increasingly, he was interested only in the news and sports. I have never been a big sports fan, and the repetitive news of CNN was numbing.

So rather than go stir crazy, I revived my old knitting obsession, a habit that had come and gone over the years. I had initially been inspired by my grandmother, who was an avid knitter, making afghans, sweaters, and socks to keep her brood of nine children and fifty-one grandchildren clothed and warm. She kept it up nearly until the day she died, just shy of one hundred years old, and I still have one of her gems, which I received at age twenty; it is a very tidy little blue cardigan that barely fit then and hardly fits now. When my daughter was young, she and I would "co-knit" scarves that were more about process than product. Over the year that I cared for my father, knitting became my therapy. I began to knit the moment I left my house for Boston Logan International Airport and continued until the end of my return flight home.

A memoir that I had found—Kyoko Mori's, *Yarn: Remembering the Way Home*—captures lessons the author learned from her knitting experience. I was most touched by her recognition that mistakes are okay. I realize that this sounds pretty basic. But somehow knitting lends itself to metaphors that speak to the heart. For example, individual pieces of yarn woven together create something beautiful and new. Or another: Sometimes, when you make too many mistakes, you just need to undo what you've done and start over. Or this one: When a ball of yarn gets really knotted, it takes a long time to undo the knots. That one captured my complex feelings toward my father, as the process of caring for him allowed me to undo the knots in our relationship.

Once I got the knitting bug, I discovered a world of knitting addicts who find pleasure, as do I, in color and texture and in crafting usable objects that people want to wear. What a concept! I also discovered that the process of knitting is meditative, relaxing, invigorating, all-consuming, jitter-reducing, anxiety-protecting, and creative. Once you've gotten past stage one, you can actually talk and knit, which is also incredibly satisfying.

I began making hats for my family, particularly my father and everyone in his caregiving sphere. First, I made four hats for each of the cousins who housed me during my visits. They called them their "Mindys." Then I created a series of five hats for my immediate family, including my husband and sister. A couple of the hats were lost, so I happily made new ones. And finally, I made a hat for my father, who, after seeing all of this knitting action, said "I'd like a Mindy." It touched me that he was joining in. The next ten or so hats were for the amazing people who cared for my father nearly 24/7, keeping him alive with their love and attention, and on and on the knitting addiction continued, filling the dual purpose of keeping people's heads warm and keeping my fidgetiness in check.

When we buried my father, my sister and I briefly considered putting his "Mindy" back on his head. But we weren't sure who we were doing it for, and it seemed a little maudlin.

Another stress reliever was writing my blog, *Mindy's Muses*, which gave me an outlet to process the overwhelming experiences of caregiving. There I discovered the universal aspects of my experience, and once again, I did not feel so alone.

Hospice

Dying can be unpredictable, especially as the body fades and the parts wear out. Sometimes it is sudden. With my mother, one massive stroke was followed shortly by a second massive stroke, and before we had time to figure out contingencies to care for her, she was gone. We could have predicted her terrible demise, given a life of depression, cigarette smoking, and excessive alcohol. But we didn't allow ourselves to imagine her death.

With my beloved aunt, a feisty, hearty woman who stayed active in civic associations well into her eighties and cooked a mean casserole, it was a total surprise. One day she began to complain that she was tired, and a few months later, she was diagnosed with melanoma and shortly thereafter died peacefully in her own home. I happened to be in the room when my aunt gasped her last breath and gurgled. It is a sound I will never forget, and it haunted me for years. Call it denial, or shortsightedness, but I wasn't ready to say goodbye to her, even though she said she was ready. This lack of preparation left me fearful about the next death. But I discovered that being involved in my father's life as he moved toward death helped gird me for the inevitable.

As his health worsened, the nurses at Harmony Village suggested that we call in hospice. He wouldn't have to leave the facility; rather, hospice nurses would come to him, checking on him regularly. The nurses at Harmony Village explained that he would no longer receive any medication that would prolong his life, although he would receive palliative care, which would keep him comfortable and out of pain without providing any life-saving treatment. Feeling panicked that we may lose him soon, I put the word out to his friends.

Our ace in the hole for communicating with the widest possible network was Darlene, an actress and director of Theatre for Change, an improvisational theater company and, equally important, a hub within the Buffalo theater community. I knew I could count on Darlene to send out the smoke signals, and almost immediately, I could tell she had worked her magic; I began to receive a steady stream of phone calls and e-mail messages from many of my father's theater friends who wanted to see him before he died.

People who were otherwise busy made time in their lives to stop by. Instead of getting quieter, my father's social life was suddenly busy again. Contrary to our expectations, he found yet another wind, as he once again basked in the attention of those around him. Who had time to die when you're surrounded by your friends? Some days he was talkative and engaged. Other days, he was quiet and removed. As for me, I was grateful once again that I was not alone; rather, I had the company of an entire community of people who cared about my father and shared in my grief. The nurses continued to come in three times a day to administer his eye medications. And the aides continued to come in every morning to weigh him, still calibrating whether or not he had too much fluid in his body. His oxygen tank still rumbled, and the mini-canisters continued to accompany him everywhere he went. He continued to take two exercise classes each day with Lorna, although some days, he petered out before the class was done and just sat there with his eyes closed as others flexed their legs and arms and played balloon volleyball. On those days when he couldn't stay awake, he berated himself for not exercising enough. He even played dice occasionally, although that short-lived interest seemed to be on the wane. Life seemed pretty normal, if there is such a thing at this stage.

For many people—including me—dying is a frightening proposition. Visiting my father could not have been easy for many of his old friends, especially those who continued to rely on him for his sage advice and practical wisdom. I imagine that those who believe in a life after death are better able to cope. And maybe it's simpler for those whose spiritual beliefs define a continuance of one's core. But for those who lack a religious or spiritual or even humanistic framework to cushion the blow, it's pretty scary. Moreover, for many people, the act of being with a dying person is emotionally charged. Certainly, there is no formula for how to behave, no script to follow, no guarantee that the dying person will even acknowledge the visitor's presence or engage in dialogue.

So how should one "be"? Is it a time to profess one's deepest feelings toward the dying person? Is it a time to simply be in the room to show one's love and caring? How does one's history with the dying person affect their final days together? Does it create more connection? Does it make it harder to connect? These are tough questions. My best guess is that expectations should be kept low and that being a presence in the room and nothing more is probably all that is needed to let the dying person know he or she is loved.

What makes matters more confounding is that it's often hard to predict when a person will die. It's something that I wanted to know and didn't want to know. Would it be days? Months? A year or more? As much as I wanted a definitive answer, I learned that there isn't an airtight timetable. So many people, including my father, defy predictions about their longevity.

As the gatekeeper for visitors, I discovered that my father had strong opinions about who he did and did not want to see. For those he had known for a long time, his answer was always "Yes." But with admirers who didn't really know him, it could go either way. Sometimes he would say, "Why not?" as if there were nothing to lose, but more often than not, he said, "No." In such cases, I could see that the energy required to respond to these visitors' hopes and expectations took too much out of him.

One of his protégés, an actor and teacher, called to say that he had a group of theater friends who wanted to institute a regular lunch date with my father at Harmony Village. We picked Mondays, and pretty soon, the weekly luncheon was called "Mondays with Manny," a take-off on the play, *Tuesdays with Morrie*, in which my father had played the lead character. The group was tickled by the name they had chosen for their weekly get-togethers. Anyone was welcome, but a core of six or so friends were regulars, coming every week without fail.

"Mondays with Manny" was a casual affair. Someone picked up sandwiches, and the group sat in one of the facility's activity rooms and chatted. In the beginning, my father was his old self, opinionated and strong. But, increasingly, he spoke less. His friends began to wonder if he was still listening, and then he surprised them all by saying something that was insightful, clear, and on target. They were momentarily relieved because his mind was still sharp. For my father, simply being in the company of his theater friends was an elixir. They were—after all—theater people who loved a good drama, and with this weekly luncheon at Harmony Village, they had hit the jackpot. They were lively and dynamic, creative and warm, and they loved him dearly. The more I saw of these friends, the more I loved them, too.

As people age and become frailer, getting out "into the world" is harder, but "Mondays with Manny" brought the outside world in. These lunches went on for about three months. I learned that some people can be in hospice for six months to a year. There are even people for whom hospice is discontinued because the life sentence is temporarily halted. We never got to that point.

As I watched and facilitated "Mondays with Manny," I learned a lesson about engaged aging and the value of intergenerational friendships. I will forever be grateful to these and other friends who held my father, literally and figuratively, until the end of his life, helping him to maintain his sense of identity until he died.

One morning, I got a call from the head nurse at Harmony Village, telling me that my father had taken a bad fall during the night. She reported that nothing was broken and that, although he appeared a bit shocked, he was still maintaining his routine, going to meals and exercise classes. Zora came in that night, after a night off, and she called me to say that he didn't look good. As I wrote at the beginning of this book, I was in Kansas, preparing to conduct a training session for a group of teachers and teaching artists. Zora and I stayed in touch, and she reported that he seemed to be picking up steam. He was just a little sleepier than usual, but the nurse assured me that this is typical after a fall. The following night, I received the call from the caregiver who was with him that evening. Within three hours, he was gone.

Death

Writing about the final year of my father's life was one way to keep him alive. Writing about his death was perhaps one way to say a final goodbye. But I resisted telling this part of the story. It's far too final, and anyway, isn't it obvious? The protagonist dies. Case closed. But I could not take the easy out. I knew that my father's death had given me a window into our relationship and into his connections with the hundreds of people he touched over the years.

My connection to him was primal. Until I reached my thirties, I believe that I loved him too much, and sadly, no other partner in my life could live up to him. Once I began to better understand him and our relationship, I found too much fault in him. I suppose this period of criticism gave me the space to "individuate" and become "my own person," separate from the person he wanted me to be.

Once I began to find my own voice and to discover my own interests and strengths, I was gradually able to see him as a whole person, with all his strengths and flaws. Still, I was often caught between wanting his approval and love and feeling annoyed with his opinionated self-absorption and narcissism. I learned, from watching him over the years, that sometimes people may achieve an impressive level of success and still feel empty. This was one of the tragedies of my father.

Caring for a parent at life's end-stage is the final sacrifice for an adult child. The key, I found, is how to give without giving away one's own being. I would guess that many of us enter this territory with mixed emotions about our parents, yet we feel we must "do the right thing" to help them end their lives in dignity. Although caring for a parent is certainly not a requirement of living, it seems like the natural thing to do. They cared for us when we were young and vulnerable, and we do the same for them when they are old and vulnerable. Gerontology researchers call this *exchange theory*. But not all adult children can do it. Maybe they were harmed too deeply during childhood, or maybe being so close at the end feels too raw.

Although my father was a flawed individual, we had a deep emotional connection at a fundamental level. I knew that at his core, he felt very alone in the world, and I felt compelled to be present for him in his final chapter. To my relief, I discovered that I was more able to love my father unconditionally, recognizing all that we had in common and acknowledging all the ways in which we were very different. Some may simply call this process "growing up," and yes, that was part of it. But I had many adult years to struggle with the difficulties in our relationship so that, by the time he finally died, I understood him and respected him, despite—and maybe in ways, because of—his and my own frailties and struggles.

I am lucky that my father lived a very long and productive life. It gave him enough time to reap the benefits of all his hard work. And, for me, it was an easier exit. I am also lucky that we both foresaw his exit many years before he died and said "I love you" at least twice a day, every day as though it were the last time. I know that sounds corny, but it sustained me for many years. When it was finally time to bury him, I suppose that I was ready, or as ready as one can be.

My father was an atheist, but he was brought up in the Jewish Orthodox tradition. We knew that the last thing he would want was a traditional Jewish funeral. But he was proud to be a Jew, and we knew that he would be happy to be buried in accordance with Reform Jewish principles, as long as we didn't get carried away! Following that tradition, he was buried as soon as family members were able to get to Buffalo for the funeral. We had no idea how many people, among friends and family members, would come at such short notice. Perhaps I shouldn't have been surprised, though—given the webs of connections he had in so many different worlds—when hundreds of people streamed into the sanctuary. And I was overwhelmed with the amount of love in that room.

I am grateful that my nephew's wife, who is more knowledgeable about Jewish religious protocol than any of us, primed us in the ritual of greeting guests as they entered. Standing in a room just off the sanctuary, we formed a receiving line, and one by one, my sister and her husband, and my husband, daughter, and I hugged and comforted hundreds of people from the many worlds my father inhabited. There were friends from the theater world, colleagues from various nonprofit boards he had been on, fellow labor activists, and even the bevy of caregivers who had tended to his needs over the past year. Many of his friends were sobbing as they told us stories about how they knew him and the ways in which he supported them. This pattern of giving is what struck me the most. The admiration for my father was intrinsically linked to his gifts of friendship and support.

Many people, as they age, seek to make their mark by sharing their wisdom and mentoring others. While my father's early life focused on standing up for his beliefs—throughout the many years he was persecuted for his political beliefs—the person he had become was far more selfless. That is the person his friends and family mourned. That is the person he had become to his friends in his final segment of his life. Instead of feeling burdened, I felt that I could have continued the greeting ritual for hours.

Now, as I reflect on this experience, I am struck by how much my attention was focused on everyone else's needs, rather than on my own. Even though I was the daughter who had lost her father, I was consoling my father's friends and colleagues. And I did not resent it one bit. Instead, I found the experience strengthening, as I absorbed the love of my father's friends, making me feel not so alone in my loss. I also felt that just a little bit of what he provided for them was being passed on to me, as I maintained the link they had to him.

After what seemed like hours, someone nudged us and said we needed to move into the main sanctuary. The night before, my sister and I had met with the young Reform Jewish Rabbi who would be conducting the service. He had never met or even heard of my father, so we had to give him a crash course in "Manny." That day, the rabbi did just enough, respecting my father's desire for a secular service, sharing a few stories we had told him, and of course, reading my father's favorite line of poetry, "Do not go gentle into that good night," by Dylan Thomas.

When I got up to speak, I looked over the crowd of expectant faces waiting for a touch of Manny's daughters to fill the room. It was enough to take my breath away. And then I spoke. Mostly I tried to summarize a few lessons I had learned from my father, like "when you fall down, you get up," his old adage to persevere in the face of challenges. But perhaps my favorite that day was "good enough," his advice when I felt overwhelmed by some task or venture. That day, I reminded myself that the words I shared with this loving, receptive group of friends would not be perfect, but they would be "good enough."

Leaving Harmony Village

With every death at Harmony Village, the assisted living community shifts, knowing that one of their own is gone, bringing the residents ever closer to their own demise. When my family went back to Harmony Village to collect my father's belongings, I mostly wanted to thank the amazing staff for making his final year as positive as it could be. There was only so much they could do, and I felt they did it beautifully. It was eerie to be back in the building, one that had become his home for the past year.

As I walked through the hallways, a few women offered their condolences. But they hadn't really known him very well. My father didn't allow anyone at Harmony Village to get too close. Except for Bones, with whom he made the closest connection. I wanted to find Bones and his partner, Lilly, but I suppose I was also afraid to see them. Whenever I spoke with Bones, he wanted reassurance that my father's health was strong. What would I say to him? Bones was nowhere to be found, so I was spared that final meeting.

As my sister and I were contemplating what we would take with us from the apartment, one of the residents, Walter, slowly and painstakingly walked into the room and, as he leaned against his cane, asked what we were doing with my father's couch. My sister and I looked at one another and immediately knew that we wanted Walter to have it. He seemed delighted, and we recruited a small group of people with strong backs to move the couch down the hallway to his room. And as Walter plunked down on the couch and sighed, he looked at me, and candidly said, "I've been wanting that couch for a long time." I silently chuckled. Here was this guy, waiting for my dad to die so he could have the damn couch! Who knew we had a vulture in our midst? But I was glad to make him happy.

I realized that the one person I felt the most sad to leave behind was Zora, who cared for my father full time for nearly a year. A paid caregiver is not an official part of the family, but she had become a part of ours. It could have been awkward, sharing the care with her, spending hours and hours together on some weekends. But Zora is a professional. Somehow, she has figured out not only how to make the end of life easier for the dying person but also how to make the family comfortable with her presence, and ultimately she felt like a part of our family. We remained in regular contact with her for about a year, until she and we moved on, but I know that at any time, we could pick up where we left off.

Carrying Forward

There are times when I wish I could talk to my father, usually when I want his opinion about something political, or when I've had a vexing interaction involving friends or family that he could help me better understand. In those moments, I yearn for the wisdom of his years. He was good at sorting things out, making me feel not so alone with my complicated emotions. At times, we were two peas in a pod, like-minded souls, struggling through the daily grind of human frailty, my own and his, and yet survivors to the finish. His former girlfriend once told me that the two of us were totally alike, except that I was nicer. It was a compliment that I didn't exactly want, except that I knew precisely what she meant. My father struggled in intimate relationships; he was an impressive public figure, but had difficulty being close. This was tough on my mother, and it was tough on other women who came into his life. In contrast, I need to connect with others and have spent a lifetime weaving together a circle of friends.

When it came to expressing his emotions, my father was frustratingly stuck. No doubt, he was a product of an era when a man's worth was measured by his ability to hold his feelings inside. But maybe he didn't get enough love and attention as a child, a boy lost amidst a gaggle of siblings who were all competing for airtime. Whatever the cause, his public charisma hid a deep well of private insecurities. And more often than not, a gruffer exterior prevailed, as he triumphed amidst the fallout from the HUAC days and the challenges of making his mark as a writer and actor.

I believe that those who persisted in getting to know my father recognized his internal struggles because they were universal struggles. Perhaps they also gleaned some strength from seeing a man who could accomplish so much and yet struggle so humanly with profound issues and questions of self-esteem. The older he got, the more accessible he became to others, and the more he appreciated those who remained solidly by his side. As I ventured into the all-encompassing universe in which I sacrificed priorities in my life to care for him, I found it easier than I had expected to be there for him. I appreciated his mellowing and was able to put in perspective some of his unsavory characteristics, recognizing that I was a lucky daughter to have been loved so unconditionally, albeit by a flawed human. Because aren't we all, in our own ways, flawed?

By being the person who helped him feel less alone as he faded toward death, I too felt less alone, recognizing at the same time that death is a solitary proposition. Taking care of my father in his final year brought me closer to my own strengths as his daughter, preparing me for this time—now—when I can stand strong without him physically by my side. I did my very best to make his life livable until the very end, and that, in and of itself, was an accomplishment. In writing this book, I suppose I have managed to keep him alive in my mind and heart, to internalize his essence so that I can carry on.

WE ARE IN THE DINING ROOM AT HARMONY VILLAGE. I tell my father that Bones is waving, and he smiles, recognizing that he has a friend at Harmony Village. He remembers that Bones is a trombone player and that many years ago, he was in a band that played at the Park Lane. Bones is used to performing, and suddenly, amidst the quiet of the room, he shouts, "Does anyone know the song, 'Unforgettable'?" My father, until that moment, seemingly caught in his own world, starts singing loudly and with great confidence and charm, "*Unforgettable, that's what you are. . . .*"

Bones shouts back at him, "Go, Mack!" And my father, not missing a beat, continues singing. His eyes are closed as he sings, and I imagine that he is transporting himself somewhere beyond the confines of this room. When I think that he will stop, he continues, and does so until the last line of the song. The room is silent, all eyes on him, but he sees no one. He is on his personal stage, singing with passion and perhaps a little tongue-in-cheek—because he knows he has a lousy voice—singing this song that harkens back to another era when he was not alone.

"That's why, darling, it's incredible, that someone so unforgettable, thinks that I am unforgettable too."

The dining room has become his theater, and the audience is frozen for a precious, bloated moment, just soaking it in. His voice is a bit off-key, but it doesn't really matter because his confidence and comfort as a performer shines through. The crowd erupts into applause, and my father smiles. He cannot see the people smiling at him, but hopefully his hearing aid is adjusted properly so he can hear their applause. For a moment, a magic moment, he is alive.

Rhoda and Manny's wedding photo, 1941

Rhoda and Manny, summer 1943

Fried family with all nine siblings and parents,
Manny on far left, circa 1950

Family photo with Manny and Rhoda, Mindy, and sister, Lorrie, 1952

Manny reading *Buffalo News* to Mindy, 1952

Mindy and Rhoda doing dishes, 1953

360 Delaware Avenue
Buffalo 2, N.Y.
April 14, 1954

Dr. Albert Einstein
Princeton University
Princeton, N.J.

Dear Dr. Einstein:

On Friday, April 9th, I was called to testify in Albany, New York, before a subcommittee of the House Committee on Un-American Activities.

I refused to answer any of their questions. Instead, I challenged the constitutionality of the committee itself.

I would like you to know that I feel very indebted to you because your position regarding what witnesses should do when called before the committee had a great influence in helping me make my own decision.

I think you will be glad to hear that the position you took has received a good response from the many working people I am in constant contact with. I myself have received the most wonderful kind of expressions of support from our union members since I refused to answer any of the questions of the committee and challenged its very right to exist.

The April 10th edition of the New York Times carried a brief report about my refusal to answer questions and my challenge concerning the committee. In an effort to break the curtain of silence which seems to have dropped since then, I have sent out a letter to a number of newspaper editors, and I enclose a copy of this letter.

Late last Friday night a newspaper reporter told me that the chairman of the subcommittee had released a statement to the press that he was recommending that I be cited for contempt for refusing to answer any questions, but I have heard nothing further on this matter.

Thank you for your inspiration. I hope I am able to do something to help stop the forces of fascism which are trying to destroy our country.

Sincerely

Emanuel J. Fried, International Representative
United Electrical, Radio & Machine Workers of America (UE)

Manny's letter to Albert Einstein, 1954. Einstein replied to Manny, "You did the right thing . . . under difficult circumstances."

Have You Seen This Man?

HE is a Communist. His name is MANNY FRIED. HE has red hair. HE wears glasses. HE is a COMMUNIST PARTY MEMBER. HE has been identified by sworn testimony before Congressional Committees as a Communist.

HAS HE BEEN IN YOUR HOUSE? If he calls on you, remember, he is a COMMUNIST, an enemy of America.

He now tries to appear respectable because he works for the I.A.M. The I.A.M. is the other Union trying to organize you. If you should vote for the I.A.M. and pay dues to I.A.M. you would be paying wages to this COMMUNIST, MANNY FRIED.

Remember, the I.A.M. (called the Machinist Union) has COMMUNISTS on their payroll.

SO BE WISE. organize into I.U.E., the Union dedicated to drive the Communists out of the labor movement.

Support I.U.E., the Union which has more G.E. emloyees as members than all other Unions combined!

DON'T PAY WAGES to America's enemies with your dues dollars.

This man is a Communist. He is on the PAYROLL of the I.A.M.

Issued by I.U.E.
502 Prudential Bldg.
28 Church St., Buffalo, N. Y.

JOIN I. U. E.

SIGN THE ATTACHED CARD

I.U.E. flyer distributed in 1956 accusing Manny of being a Communist

BU 100-802

Confidential

FRIED stated that if he did not hear regarding his, FRIED's resignation from the U.E. Staff, he was going to enroll in school. (Furnished to on September 5, 1949)

stated that MANNY FRIED was lining up people for the U.E. Convention in Cleveland, Ohio. (Furnished to on September 14, 1949)

MANNY FRIED was back in the U.E. in the Tonawandas. (Furnished to on September 22, 1949)

(Furnished to on September 26, 1949)

On November 2, 1949, the Buffalo Evening News carried an article which tells of U.E. Field Representative, EMANUEL FRIED, who scoffed at a statement made in Cleveland by CIO Regional Director HUGH THOMPSON that practicall

-4-

Confidential

One sample from the five thousand heavily redacted pages from the FBI files on Manny, 1948

Manny at a Jobs with Justice rally, 1994

Manny teaching Writers Workshop for delegates of Metro Toronto Labor Council, 1985

Rhoda painting a portrait of a union member, 1950s

Rhoda's portrait of José, waiter at the Park Lane Restaurant, 1970

Rhoda's portrait of Manny's mother (Mindy's grandmother), circa 1965

Rhoda's self-portrait, approximately age 45

Cast, *Taming of the Shrew*, Federal Theatre Traveling Company, 1932 (Manny, far right, standing in front row, age 21)

Actors carrying placards in Manny's play *Rose*, Provincetown Playhouse, New York City, 1982 (Manny, not pictured, was 69 at the time)

OPPOSITE: *Drop Hammer*, Manny's play performed at Los Angeles Actors Theatre, 1980 (age 67)

Henry IV, Buffalo Shakespeare in the Park, 1991, with actors Tom Martin, Manny (age 78), and Richard Wesp

OPPOSITE: Manny (age 95) at Fried family reunion, 2007. Photo by Paul Pitts

"Command Central" at Harmony Village, 2010.
Photo by Paul Pitts

Notes

CHAPTER 1

1. See *buffalo.com/2015/04/25/news/theater/theater-previews/spirit-of-manny-fried-lives-on-at-subversive-theatre* for front headline of the *Buffalo News*.
2. FBI files, Emanuel Fried.
3. FBI files, Emanuel Fried.
4. Participant at "Red Diaper Baby Conference." (World Fellowship Center, N. Conway, New Hampshire, 1982).
5. The names of assisted living residences, residents, and professional care providers have been changed to protect their privacy, and any additional fictitious names are identified where they appear.
6. See *www.ahcancal.org/ncal/Pages/index.aspx*, and *www.ahcancal.org/ncal/about/Documents/GPAssistedLiving.pdf.*

CHAPTER 4

1. See, for example, *www.ahcancal.org/ncal/resources/Pages/ResidentProfile.aspx* and *www.cdc.gov/nchs/data/databriefs/db91.pdf.*
2. Forage Bookstore and Howard are fictitious names.

Bibliography

Atchley, Robert C. "Continuity Theory of Normal Aging." *The Gerontologist* 29, no. 2 (1989): 183–90.

"Average Costs for Long Term Care Insurance Rise 8.6 Percent," *American Association for Long-Term Care Insurance*, January 27, 2015, *www.aaltci.org/news/long-term-care-insurance-association-news/average-costs-for-long-term-care-insurance-rise-8-6-percent.*

Bernstein, Carl. Loyalties: *A Son's Memoir*. New York: Simon and Schuster, 1989.

Brown, Jeffrey R., and Amy Finkelstein. "Insuring Long-Term Care in the United States." *The Journal of Economic Perspectives* 25, no. 4 (2011): 119–41.

Butler, Robert N. *Why Survive? Being Old in America*. Baltimore: Johns Hopkins University Press, 1975.

Caarns, A. "Long-Term Care Insurance: Costs Are Up but Vary Widely." *New York Times*, February. 9, 2015. *www.nytimes.com/2015/02/21/your-money/long-term-care-insurance-costs-are-up-but-vary-widely.html?emc=eta1.*

Caffrey, Christine, Manisha Sengupta, Eunice Park-Lee, Abigail Moss, Emily Rosenoff, and Lauren Harris-Kojetin. "Residents Living in Residential Care Facilities: United States, 2010." *NCHS Data Brief*, no. 91 (April 2012).

"Caregiving in the U.S." *National Alliance for Caregiving and AARP*, 2004.

"Caregiving in the U.S." *National Alliance for Caregiving and AARP*, 2009.

"Caregiving in the U.S." *National Alliance for Caregiving and AARP*, 2012.

Cole, Thomas, and Sally Gadow, eds., *What Does It Mean to Grow Old? Reflections from the Humanities*. Durham: Duke University Press, 1987.

"Consumer Information Guide: Assisted Living Residence," *New York State Department of Health*, [n.d.], *www.health.ny.gov/publications/1505.pdf*.

Cumming, Elaine, and William Henry. *Growing Old*. New York: Basic Books Publishing, 1961.

Eckert, Kevin, Paula Carder, Leslie Morgan, Ann Christine Frankowski, and Erin Roth. *Inside Assisted Living: The Search for Home*. Baltimore: Johns Hopkins University Press, 2009.

Fried, Mindy, and Claire Reinelt. "I Am This Child's Mother: A Feminist Perspective on Mothering with a Disability." In *Families in the U.S.: Kinship and Domestic Policies*, edited by Karen V. Hansen and Anita Ilta Garey, 339–48. Philadelphia: Temple University Press, 1998.

Friedan, Betty. *The Fountain of Age*. New York: Simon and Schuster, 1993.

"Growth in Long-Term Care Costs Slows." Prudential Financial Report. *Professional Services Close-Up*, September 28, 2010.

Gubrium, Jaber. *Living and Dying at Murray Manor*. Charlottesville: University Press of Virginia, 1997.

Gubrium, Jaber, and James Holstein. *Aging and Everyday Life*. Malden, MA: Blackwell, 2000.

"Guiding Principles," *National Center for Assisted Living*, 2014, *www.ahcancal.org/ncal/about/Documents/GPAssistedLiving.pdf*.

Havighurst, R. J. "Successful Aging." *The Gerontologist* 1 (1961).

Howdlewsky, R. Tamara. "Staffing Problems and Strategies in Assisted Living." In *Assisted Living: Needs, Practices, and Policies in Residential Care for the Elderly*, edited by Sheryl Zimmerman, Philip D. Sloane, and J. Kevin Eckert, 78–91. Baltimore: Johns Hopkins University Press, 2001.

Kane, Rosalie A., Jane Chan, and Robert L. Kane. "Assisted Living Literature Through May 2004: Taking Stock." *The Gerontologist* 47, no. 6 (2007): 125.

Kaufman, Sharon R. *The Ageless Self: Sources of Meaning in Late Life*. Madison: University of Wisconsin Press, 1985.

———. "The Ageless Self." In *Aging in Everyday Life*, edited by Gubrium and Holstein. New York: Wiley-Blackwell, 2000.

Kayser-Jones, Jeannie. *Old, Alone, and Neglected: Care of the Aged in Scotland and the United States*. Berkley: University of California Press, 1990.

Kemp, Candace L., Shanzhen Luo, and Mary M. Ball. "Meds Are a Real Tricky Area: Examining Medication Management and Regulation in Assisted Living." *Journal of Applied Gerontology* 31, no. 1 (2012): 126–49.

Linde, Paul. *Of Spirits and Madness: An American Psychiatrist in Africa.* New York: McGraw Hill, 2002.

Loe, Meika. *Aging Our Way: Lessons for Living from 85 and Beyond.* New York: Oxford University Press, 2011.

"Long Term Care Options," *Assisted Living Federation of America*, 2013, *www.alfa.org/alfa/Senior_Living_Options.asp.*

Lyons, Paul. *Philadelphia Communists, 1936–1956.* Philadelphia: Temple University Press, 1982.

Matos, Kenneth, and Ellen Galinsky. "2014 National Study of Employers," *Families and Work Institute, familiesandwork.org/downloads/2014NationalStudyOfEmployers.pdf.*

McGowin, Diana Friel. *Living in the Labyrinth: A Personal Journey Through the Maze of Alzheimer's.* New York: Dell Publishing, 1993.

"Medicaid's Assisted Living Benefits: Availability and Eligibility." *The American Elder Care Research Organization*, updated April 2015, *www.payingforseniorcare.com/medicaid-waivers/assisted-living.html#title1.*

"Medication Management in Assisted Living." Washington, DC: Center for Excellence in Assisted Living, 2007.

"The Metlife Study of Employer Costs for Working Caregivers," 1997, *www.caregiving.org/data/employercosts.pdf.*

"The MetLife Study of Employer Costs for Working Caregivers," June 1997, *www.caregiving.org/data/employercosts.pdf.*

Mitty, Ethel L. "Assisted Living and the Role of Nursing." Policy Perspectives. *American Journal of Nursing* 103, no. 8 (2003): 32.

———. "Medication Management in Assisted Living: A National Survey of Policies and Practices." *Journal of the American Medical Directors Association* 10 (2009): 107–14.

Mollica, R. L. "State Medicaid Reimbursement Policies and Practices in Assisted Living." Prepared for American Health Care Association and National Center for Assisted Living, 2009.

Moody, Harry R. "The Meaning of Life and the Meaning of Old Age." In *What Does It Mean to Grow Old? Reflections from the Humanities*, edited by Thomas Cole and Sally Gadow. Durham: Duke University Press, 1987.

———. *Aging Concepts and Controversies*, 6th ed. Thousand Oaks, CA: Pine Forge, 2010.

Mulvey, Janemarie. "Factors Affecting the Demand for Long-Term Care Insurance: Factors for Congress." Congressional Research Service (2012).

Newman, Katherine. *A Different Shade of Gray: Midlife and Beyond in the Inner City.* New York: New Press, 2006.

"Northwestern Mutual Releases Study Detailing Long-Term Care Costs by State." *Professional Services Close-Up*, December 10, 2012, *www.northwesternmutual.com/about-us/studies/cost-of-long-term-care-study*.

Ortman, Jennifer, Victoria Velkoff, and Howard Hogan. "An Aging Nation: The Older Population in the United States." US Census Bureau [May, 2014].

Pitt-Catsouphes, Marcie, Christina Matz-Costa, and Elyssa Bessen. Age and Generations: Understanding Experiences at the Workplace. Sloan Center on Aging and Work, 2009, *www.bc.edu/content/dam/files/research_sites/agingandwork/pdf/publications/RH06_Age_Generations.pdf*.

Quadagno, Jill. *Aging and the Life Course*, 5th ed. New York: McGraw Hill, 2011.

"Resident Profile." *National Center for Assisted Living*, 2010, *www.ahcancal.org/ncal/resources/Pages/ResidentProfile.aspx*.

Rowe, John, and Robert Kahn. "Successful Aging." *The Gerontologist* 37 (4): 433–40. doi: *10.1093/geront/37.4.433*.

Schwarz, B., and Ruth Brent. *Aging, Autonomy, and Architecture: Advances in Assisted Living*. Baltimore: Johns Hopkins University Press, 1999.

"Two Thousand Nine Overview of Assisted Living," *Assisted Living Federation of America*, *www.alfa.org/Mall/StoreHome.asp?MODE=VIEW&STID=1&LID=0&PRODID=16*.

Wise, Meg, Lucille Marchand, James F. Cleary, Elizabeth Aeschlimann, and Daniel Causier. "Integrating a Narrative Medicine Telephone Interview with Online Life Review Education for Cancer Patients: Lessons Learned and Future Directions." *Journal of the Society for Integrative Oncology* 7, no. 1 (2009): 19.

Young, H., S. Gray, W. S. McCormick, S. Sikma, S. Reinhard, L. Johnson Trippett, and T. Allen. "Types, Prevalence, and Potential Clinical Significance of Medication Administration Errors in Assisted Living." *Journal of the American Geriatrics Society* 56, no. 7 (2008): 1199–205.

Zimmerman, S., K. Love, L. W. Cohen, P. D. Sloane, and the CEAL-UNC Partnership. Research Brief. "Medication Administration in Assisted Living." Chapel Hill: University of North Carolina, 2009.

Zimmerman, Sheryl, Philip D. Sloane, and J. Kevin Eckert, eds. *Assisted Living: Needs, Practices, and Policies in Residential Care for the Elderly*. Baltimore: Johns Hopkins University Press, 2001.

Index